W9-CCG-774

Carol Showalter

PARACLETE PRESS
BREWSTER, MASSACHUSETTS

20 19 18 17 16 15 14 13 12 11 10 9

Copyright © 1977 by Carol Showalter
ISBN #: 0-941478-05-X
Library of Congress Catalog #:77-90947
All rights reserved.
Published by Paraclete Press
Brewster, Massachusetts
www.paraclete-press.com

Printed in the United States of America.

Cover Design: Timothy Showalter Graphic Designs
Cover Photography: Timothy Showalter

In gratitude to God for all His blessings to me

and with loving thanks to
my husband, Dr. William Showalter
my children, Timothy, Elizabeth, Peter and Helen
my brother, Brian, who was like a son to me, and his family
my grandchildren, Sandra, William, Andrea and Alison Marie
and my very close Christian family at the Community of Jesus

Surely goodness and mercy have followed me
all the days of my life . . .

Preface

Twenty-five years ago I was the young wife of a minister, the mother of three small children—and a perpetually frustrated dieter. As I was about to enroll for the third or fourth time in a well-known diet program that met in our church, God spoke to me in a most extraordinary way: through a hand-painted sign on a Sunday School wall. The message was this: "God HAS the answer."

Now, I wasn't convinced that God was at all interested in my frustrations, whether they were with my role as a minister's wife and mother, or with my problem of being overweight. My understanding of God—or more accurately, my *misunderstanding* of Him—was of a judge who watched from on high, expecting me to stay on top of things and be good at everything I did.

On this particular day I felt like a failure. After all, I was a graduate of a famous diet program, and I knew how to eat, what to eat, and when to eat—but I was failing AGAIN. So when I read that Sunday School sign, its words hit deep inside me. At that very moment I made a decision to believe that God does indeed have the answer, and that He is very much aware of my needs. I did not sign up for that diet program, but instead walked out of the room knowing God was going to touch the needs of my life. I wasn't mistaken.

I marvel at the love, mercy, and understanding of our God. He began to bring healing to my struggle with weight, but very soon He was touching all areas of my life. A small group of other women in the church joined me, women who were looking for honest, open relationships to deal with problems in their lives. Soon they found themselves caring for one another and—with God's help—supporting each other with their personal, daily problems. Not only did their own lives change, but their families and fellow church members found their lives blessed.

I invite you to walk with me through the pages of this book: Laugh with me, cry with me, and believe with me that the same God who was faithful to meet my needs, has the answer for *you.* This book will start the process. Becoming a part of the 3D program in your local church, or starting a program on your own, will bless you abundantly. God *is* faithful and He *does* care about the things that bother us, whether they be problems with our diet or with things that affect our moods, our eating habits, or our family dynamic. He could have chosen anyone to deliver this message, but He used my failures and struggles to serve as an example of how He can bring His life and vitality to anyone who desires them. It is my prayer that this book will touch *your* life.

1

Smile, God Has The Answer

"Tim, Betsy," I called, looking out the window. "Get your sweaters on; the bus has just turned the corner." The route of bus #139 took it down Pixley Road, which bordered our lot, and then around the block before stopping in front of our house. It was handy. The children didn't have to wait outside, as long as I kept watch out the kitchen window.

It was becoming a beautiful fall day. The sunlight filtering through the trees in our yard in suburban Rochester, New York, was changing morning, from dark and brisk, to bright and warm. Our house was surrounded by trees, and the first dabs of orange and yellow were appearing on the tips of the leaves. I loved the fall; it reminded me of New England where I was born and raised.

Pulling his sweater over his head, Tim grabbed his bag lunch from the counter and headed for the front door. "Hey!" I said. He returned quickly to brush my cheek with a kiss, and flash a cocky smile before disappearing out the front door. Tim was nine and a half and in the fifth grade.

"Betsy!" I yelled, "You're going to miss the bus."

Unhurried footsteps indicated she was coming. I grabbed her sweater off the chair, put it on her, and propelled her towards the front door. The bus was stopping out front. "Here's your lunch—now hurry." I watched her climb on the bus, waved my final goodbye, and went back to the kitchen. My bus watch was over, but instead of finishing the dishes, I knelt on the chair, looking out the window again, this time at the church parking lot across the street.

I was startled when my husband Bill slipped his arm around me.

"Didn't mean to scare you," he said. "I just wanted to kiss you goodbye before heading over to church." He paused and looked at me. "Where are your thoughts this beautiful fall morning?"

"Oh, I don't know; just daydreaming, I guess."

"What's so inviting out there?" he asked, resting his hands on my shoulders and looking out the window. Reaching up, I put my hands on top of his and said, "Nothing, honey. I'm just nosey and wonder what's going on at church."

The moment the words came out, I felt guilty. I knew exactly what I was looking for, but I didn't want to tell him. Not yet.

"Well, okay," was his response, and he leaned down and kissed me and headed out the side door. "Don't forget it's Monday," he said over his shoulder, "and the men meet in my office for lunch. I'll need a sandwich."

"Sure, hon, I'll bring one over just before noon. Have a good day."

I turned back to the window and watched my husband walk across the yard, heading towards the stately, red brick, colonial church. Bill was the senior minister of the Parkminster Presbyterian Church, one of Rochester's rapidly growing young congregations, and our manse was directly across the street from the church. We had moved here three years ago, in September of 1969, from an inner-city parish in Bridgeport, Connecticut. I had loved Bridgeport and hated to move, but more and more I was feeling very comfortable and happy in Rochester.

My eyes were still fixed on the parking lot. In drove a big red station wagon and out stepped a big red-coated lady. A moment later, a blue compact parked beside the wagon. Its door opened; a huge lady in a raincoat struggled to get out. More cars were pulling in, and more fat ladies were getting out, all clad in coats, though the weather only called for sweaters. I knew the reason from experience: overweight people usually think a coat masks their true girth. My question of the morning was being answered right before my eyes: Weight Watchers was still meeting at our church on Monday mornings.

Now I had to face the next question: should I march myself over there and join that group today?

Just before falling asleep last night, I had promised myself that if they were still meeting, I would join. It was easy to make that promise last night. I had overeaten again at supper and then snacked on chocolate chip cookies just before I went upstairs. I was uncomfortably full. But now this morning, I was gradually convincing myself that if I really tried again to cut back, I could do it all by myself. After all, I did resist that second piece of toast at breakfast. But then, breakfast never did turn me on that much, so I knew underneath I wasn't too victorious.

I refused to talk to anyone about it, even Bill, because I couldn't bear to admit that my weight was out of control again. Last night I had finally made up my mind, but now I was fighting the reality of having to join that parade of fat women marching into the church. After all, I certainly wasn't that fat!

"Mommy?" My thoughts were interrupted by a tug at my arm. "Let's go to church," came this tiny voice. There stood my two-and-a-half-year-old son Peter. The nursery at church, where babysitting was available daily, was one of his favorite places. He could always count on a good time, with lots of friends and lots of toys.

"Okay, Peter Stephen, I guess it's time to go." His words

pushed me over the brink of indecision where I had been teetering all morning. I sighed and stood up. "Where's your jacket?" I asked, looking down at his big hazel eyes full of excitement.

He ran towards the hall closet and pointed up to his little blue corduroy jacket. I slipped it on him and zipped it up. I started to reach for my beige sweater but decided instead to wear my navy raincoat.

As we walked across the backyard, I spotted my neighbor, Mrs. Cassidy, at her window. She always made it a point to greet the children when they were out in the yard or walking over to church. I picked Peter up and pointed to her. He smiled and waved his hand furiously. She's probably noticed I've been getting fat again, I thought. Would she guess that I was headed over to the Weight Watchers meeting at church? Were any of the other neighbors looking out at Peter and me? Good Lord, what's the matter with me today? I'm practically paranoid about this weight thing. You would think I was some obese thing waddling across the yard!

Weight obsessed me. Whether I was gaining or losing, I was thinking about it most of the time. In fact, that was the first thing I noticed about other people, so I guess I was convinced that that was the first thing they noticed about me. And I'd judged overweight people for years. I was pretty proud that I could lose weight quite successfully. But I never stopped to face the cold fact that I gained weight just as successfully every year.

A very fat woman was walking into the side door of the church ahead of me and Peter. She went upstairs and I went downstairs. Ultimately we were both going to end up in the same room, but I would delay that situation a few minutes longer. I stood around the nursery long enough to settle Peter and finally trudged upstairs.

Walking into the room killed me. Fat women were all over

the place. Some were sitting down gabbing away, others were in lines waiting for one thing or another. Three women in the room, out of fifty or sixty, had decent figures. And two of these were sitting at the table registering people for class.

The class was being held in what we called the East Hall. It used to be the sanctuary of the original church, which we had outgrown, but was now used for Sunday school classes and community groups such as this. It was a good large room, with plenty of space for rows of chairs, tables for registrations and a private weigh-in area. A number of partitions were shifted around the room to set off the particular needs of the program. I took my place in the line of women waiting to register.

This weight battle had been going on in my life for such a long time—over ten years. In the course of a year I would gain twenty or twenty-five pounds, and then in two or three months I would lose them any way I could. I had tried all kinds of crash diet programs that sometimes worked and sometimes didn't. I would eat only one thing for three or four weeks and usually lose the weight pretty quickly. (I remember one time eating only beets for three weeks!) But the least painful method for me, or so I thought, was to take diet pills—prescribed amphetamines—which the teenagers called "speed."

They certainly took my desire for food away, but at the same time I would also lose close touch with reality. Talking too much and flitting nervously from one thing to another was usually a sure sign that I was into the bottle of pills again. But if Bill would question me at all, I would squirm around the subject.

"You seem awfully hyper to me," he would say. "Are you taking those darn diet pills again?"

"Why do you always blame the diet pills?" I would respond. "The real problem with me is that there is too much work that has to be done at church and around the house. Maybe if you'd get me some more help in those areas, I wouldn't be so hyper!"

That would usually cow him, and he wouldn't say any more. And I would continue to take the diet pills, until the amount of weight I had to lose was gone. This went on for at least four years. Bill did not dare say much, but I knew he was alarmed that I was so dependent on diet pills. And in the late sixties, the drug scene was getting pretty bad. I finally decided I shouldn't have those pills around the house with teenage babysitters and church groups over so often, so I flushed what I had down the toilet, vowing never to use them again. Naturally, I waited to do this until I was thin again.

Now, with the diet pills gone, and the crash diets growing less and less successful as I grew older, I knew I had to find another route to get rid of my excess weight each year. In May of 1970, I went to see my doctor for my yearly checkup.

"Mrs. Showalter?" I put my magazine down and stood up to follow a nurse with a clipboard in her hand. "Would you come this way, please?" I followed closely behind her, trying to be amiable, but she was all business. "Beautiful day, isn't it?" I suggested. No response.

She stopped abruptly at the gray monster—the hospital scale outside the doctor's office. "Please step up here, so I can check your weight for the doctor." I started to take off my shoes, but she said, "That isn't necessary, Mrs. Showalter; it won't make much difference." Well, I knew she was wrong! Shoes do make a difference and so does the time of day and several other things, but there was no sense in arguing with her. I'd just deduct in my own mind what I thought those shoes weighed and also a pound or so because it was the middle of the afternoon, and I always weighed more at that time.

The bottom weight indicator was set in the 100-pound notch. She pushed the top weight to the far right. Nothing happened; the balance bar at the end of the scale cleaved to the top— 147, 148, 150, still nothing. "Looks like we'll have to move up a notch," she remarked casually. That meant into the 150-pound notch. If only she had let me take off my shoes.

The clunk of the weight as she changed it seemed to echo all over the waiting room. I was sure everyone heard it for a mile around.

She kept moving the top weight, but still nothing happened. My eyes were glued to the balance bar; when would it detach itself from the top? Oh, no, 160, 165, and now finally a slight movement, and slowly it began to descend. I was 167½ pounds and devastated. I expected that I would be over 150, but never did I dream I was back up there—again.

My doctor was angry when he read the chart. "Get that weight off, Carol, and quickly! You're too young to weigh almost 170 pounds." I didn't say anything, but inside I was furious. Who did he think he was? I was there for my gynecological checkup, not a lecture on weight control.

"As soon as you leave here today, I want you to find the diet group nearest to your house and join it right away. Like Weight Watchers or Diet Workshop. Either of those near you?"

I dearly wished I could have lied at that point. But I paused and gulped noticeably, "Yes, Weight Watchers has two groups that meet in our church every week."

"Well, there can't be anything more convenient," he smiled. But he wouldn't just drop it. He went on to talk about how young mothers fall into depression from being overweight, and how older people literally die from overweight, and on and on.

I was insulted and angry, but his confrontation worked. The next week I joined Weight Watchers. (To my chagrin I weighed in at 167½ that first meeting-without my shoes and before breakfast!) And the program worked for me. The first twenty pounds went quickly, then I got comfortable and lazy for awhile. I thought I looked pretty good at 147, and I was not as anxious to get the rest off. In fact it wasn't until August, 1971, fifteen months after I joined, that I graduated at 130 pounds. Naturally,

I was totally convinced that I would never, never gain weight again. Finally, I knew how and what to eat. It would be easy from here on—or so I thought.

Now, in October of 1972, I was standing in line at the same Weight Watchers group, waiting to register again. The line had been moving steadily, and I was facing the thin registration clerk. She told me to fill out the front and back questions on the payment book and said the weekly fee was $2.50, in addition to a $5.00 registration fee.

"Does it make any difference that I'm a graduate of this program?" I asked quietly. (I never would have mentioned it, but I had a hunch the cost was less for ex-members.)

"Oh," she said, looking up at me, perhaps trying to remember my face. "Do you have your lifetime membership book with you?"

"No, I'm sorry, and I haven't the vaguest idea what I did with it. I hadn't planned on using it again," I mumbled.

I hated the humiliation of needing Weight Watchers, and its membership certificate was not something I treasured. I had buried it somewhere and quickly forgotten about it.

"I'll look in our files and see if we have your old registration number and weight chart, Mrs. Showalter. In the meantime, why don't you just step over to the other line and wait to be weighed in."

The line I was now in was moving towards one of the room dividers. There were voices behind the divider, but the conversations were not discernible. "Next, please," were the only words that clearly came over the top of the partition. While I was still standing there, the clerk brought me my new book. "You don't have to pay the registration fee, Mrs. Showalter," she said, handing me back a five dollar bill. "And if, I mean, when, you get within two pounds of your goal, you will no longer have to pay the weekly fee, either. Those are the privileges of our graduates," she said smiling and giving a plug for the program to those within earshot.

As I waited in line, I began to wonder where that membership book could be. . . probably with the tiny square box that said "Congratulations" on the front of it. Inside was a silver pin, with diamond chips, indicating that I was a successful graduate of the program. I never wore the pin. I wasn't about to advertise the fact that I was ever fat!

Soon the "Next, please" was for me. I stepped behind the divider and handed my book to a slender, grayhaired woman. She didn't even bother to look up. I was only a number to her. "Step on the scale, please."

"Can't I take off my shoes?" I pleaded.

"Of course," she answered, as if I should have known better than to ask. She was obviously in a hurry. There were still a dozen women behind me, waiting to be weighed.

Things hadn't changed much in the past two years. The weigher could read the weight, but the person on the scale had the numbers blocked by a large, strategically placed, piece of cardboard with a "fat" joke on it. That had always irritated me, because I wanted to know what I weighed—exactly. And I didn't trust her honesty. Besides, why should she know my weight, before I knew it? Whose body was it anyway?

"You're 147½, Mrs. Showalter," she announced.

"That's a relief! I was sure I'd be over 150," I said, trying to cheer myself up.

"Well," she replied, smiling, "it wasn't that long ago you were 130 pounds, was it?"

I groaned. How did she know? It probably was written in that exasperating little lifetime membership book. I picked up my payment book and headed out. The next lady was already behind the partition, taking off her shoes.

Choosing a seat on the end of the very last row, I noticed that the only man in the room was at the other end—a very big, fat man, reading a newspaper. Actually, he did not appear to be interested in the paper, but he seemed even less interested in talking to any of the women in the hall. I felt the same way. I too, preferred to do my socializing elsewhere. Unfortunately, I didn't have a newspaper or anything else to read, so I had to find some other way to avoid conversations. I began to look around the room for objects of interest. Bible verses were written on blackboards, and Sunday School papers were tacked up on the various partitions. One partition caught my attention: a big, red smile face was painted right on the rough finish of the partition. The face was trimmed widely with black paint and there were large bold words beside it: *Smile, God Has The Answer.*

I couldn't take my eyes off those words. Smile—I wasn't in the mood. "If God has the answer, why am I here?" I asked myself. "I feel miserable sitting in this room. But I have to get this weight off again, before I climb back up to 170." And I knew very well I was on my way; I could feel it.

That smile sign was disgustingly persistent. It made me mad. I knew God has answers for lots of problems, but He had never helped me with my weight problem! Yes, answers for searching teenagers, answers for troubled marriages, answers for big problems, but. . .

I squirmed. Hey, preacher's wife, won't your God help you? Can't you practice what you preach to so many others? The thoughts coming at me from the potent sign were like poison darts.

But I *had* prayed. Many, many nights I had prayed. Falling asleep, I would beg God to please take away my desire for the fattening S's—sweets, snacks and seconds! But I would wake up and hardly be able to wait until breakfast to take the first bite of a doughnut. Then after breakfast, I'd remember God and throw up a quick prayer, asking Him to keep all temptations away from me throughout the day, quickly quoting the verse in I Corinthians which said, "There has no temptation overtaken you but such as is common to man. But God is faithful and just and will not allow you to be tempted above that which you are able to bear. . ." Now it was up to God to just keep those temptations away from me. The responsibility was on Him. But I would bump smack into moist chocolate chip cookies, sticky sweet rolls, and filled candy dishes everywhere I turned. I couldn't resist! "If only He had kept the temptations away," I would say to myself, enjoying every bite of my "sin." I was still looking at the smile face, when a voice up front interrupted my thoughts.

"Good morning, ladies! And to our newcomers, welcome to Weight Watchers! We have been meeting here at Parkminster Church for over two years now, and every week we add new members."

The speaker was an attractive woman of about thirty-five. I had seen her buzzing around the room and assumed that she was the lecturer. She had the best figure in the room, and the way she was dressed and strutted around, it was obvious that it was a relatively new figure of which she was proud. I was jealous of it.

"Before we get too far into today's meeting," she went on, "I have something for you to see — a picture of me three summers ago." She flashed an enlarged picture of herself draped over a chaise lounge eating a piece of cake and drinking something out of a can. The fat was literally hanging off of her lifted arm, and she was bulging over the sides of the lounge. It was hard to believe that it was really her. "I've lost 106 pounds and have kept just about all of it off for almost three years now. And if I can do it, so can you!"

It was a good thing she said, "just about all of it," because I could see at least ten pounds that she shouldn't be carrying.

I looked around the room; her audience was dazzled. Those fat ladies were hungrily picturing themselves standing up front a year from now, a trim size twelve. You could see the dreams in their eyes. For the next ten minutes, she talked about the emotional and medical dangers for fat people, emphasizing her points with a hand-made flip chart, full of statistics. I was bored and tuned her out. That smile face was still grinning at me, and I was pouting back at it.

Suddenly the thought struck me: was God trying to say something to me through that sign? Perhaps half an hour had passed since I first saw that big red face, and those five words. Maybe God had an answer for me I hadn't heard before. I had no idea what it could be. The lecturer continued. Names were being called now, and an announcement of how much weight each person had lost in the week. There was laughter and clapping after each name, but I was not a part of it. I was busy making a decision.

"All new members must stay after the class for a few minutes, so that I can explain some of the details of the diet," she said, pointing to the side of the room I was sitting on. "We'll meet over there. The rest of you are free to go now. Have a good week, everyone," she said, waving goodbye.

While the majority of the ladies headed towards the door, six or seven were making their way to the rows she had pointed to. I got up and headed for the door myself. I could almost feel the lecturer's eyes on my back. At that moment I had no idea what I was going to do about my weight problem after I walked out that door. But I knew God was going to help me—somehow. He did have the answer. And as I slipped out the door, just before it closed, I was almost smiling.

I picked up Peter in the nursery, and we walked back across the parking lot and the yard to the house. I felt peaceful now. And I began to see some things about myself. I had to stop putting the blame on God for not answering my prayers. The problem was me, not God. I loved to eat—I just hated to gain weight. And even after "willing" the weight off through Weight Watchers, I still chose to begin eating the wrong foods again. And no amount of praying in the morning or at night was going to magically wash those calories away. If I ate what I wanted, when I wanted to, I was going to get fat again. It was as simple as that. The problem was not God, nor was it with the Weight Watchers program. The problem was me! And it was about time I faced that.

Those thoughts mulling around in my head were interrupted by Peter, as soon as we walked in the kitchen door. "Can I have a cookie, Mommy?" he asked, pointing up to the cookie jar. "Sure, Tiger," and I got one out for him—just one.

2

The End of a Pretend World

In the months that followed that October morning in 1972, I found that my weight problem no longer consumed my thoughts, yet at the same time I didn't try to avoid it. It seemed like the whole thing was simply de-emphasized. I was still heavier than I should have been, but I was peaceful. And something else: the compulsive eating seemed to stop. I wasn't losing, but I wasn't gaining, either. And I was able to hold it around 145 pounds.

Almost before I knew it, fall and winter had passed and spring was upon us. Spring is a time of celebration for upstate New Yorkers. The intensely cold winters are a full five months long and the first signs of spring are welcomed jubilantly with, among other things, the planning of a spring luncheon at church. So when the first buds appeared on the lilac trees, and tulips and daffodils began to push their noses through the ground, the women of the church began to plan their annual spring luncheon. The date this year would be May 3rd.

The table decorations would be as many different colors of spring flowers as could be found in the early gardens, and women from all over the community would be invited. The guest speakers: two women who were not strangers to our congregation, Mrs. Cay Andersen and Mrs. Judy Sorensen.

Bill and I had first heard Cay and Judy, as they were popularly known, twelve years earlier, in 1961, at a Faith at Work conference in Northfield, Massachusetts. They had shared how God had called them, in a little church on Cape Cod, to minister together as a team, counseling and leading retreats at various churches around New England.

Cay's husband, Bill, was a builder, and they owned and operated a beautiful guest house at Rock Harbor, near Orleans, with their son, Peter. They led a relatively peaceful life; although Cay had been a very sick woman for several years, she was now able to manage the guest house. The Sorensen family, Judy and Bill, who was a business executive, and their four children, vacationed on Cape Cod every year. Before long, the Sorensens moved in with the Andersens at Rock Harbor—four adults and five children under one roof. The teaching they had done at Northfield and at other churches was based largely on the experiences they were having in living out the Christian life under these circumstances (long before community living had gained any popular acceptance).

Our first reaction to their sharing was mixed. Bill was put off by their lack of formal Christian training, and yet he was intrigued by them. "They're so spontaneous!" I exclaimed. "They don't seem to prepare their talks, and they don't seem to know who is going to speak first or say what." We came away not quite knowing what to make of these two ladies from Cape Cod.

Then, four years later, while vacationing in New Hampshire, we found ourselves at a Christian center for three weeks, where it just happened that Cay and Judy were scheduled to lead a ten-day retreat. From the announcement, we learned that they had been doing a great deal of speaking since we had seen them in 1961, and had also become involved in the healing ministry. Only a few months before, my mother had discovered that she had an advanced case of cancer and had less than six months to live. So we called her and asked her to come to New Hampshire and join us at this retreat. She came, also anxious to hear what the healing ministry was all about, and perhaps harboring the hope that God, through these two women, might do something about her cancer. She was not quite fifty years old and had a son, four, my brother Brian, an unexpected but rich blessing to her and my dad.

We all learned a great deal about healing and about the work and power of God's Holy Spirit that week in New Hampshire. But most of all, we learned about the need to get our relationships with our families into the place where they were pleasing to God. Mom and I talked about a lot of hurts and misunderstandings we had while I was growing up, all the normal mother-daughter problems, plus a few that were uniquely our own.

There were four of us kids in the family. I was number two and the only girl. Boys generally get preferential treatment, and our home was no exception. I sized that situation up early in life. It was a man's world, and the only way to be at the center of attention was to beat my brothers. But the odds were insurmountable, and I began to employ more devious methods. I became Daddy's girl. That was something my brothers couldn't do, and it worked pretty well. I got the attention I wanted, but it was never enough. I became haunted by the conviction that my parents really *did* love my brothers more than me.

Through most of my later childhood and adolescence, I complained bitterly to my mother that she preferred the boys and would insist, whenever she tried to deny it. This instilled instant guilt in her and got me a lot of attention, while she repeatedly tried to prove to me it wasn't so. But the irony was that I myself had come to believe what had initially been a ploy for attention. With the result that I gradually became obsessed by a craving for acceptance and a corresponding fear of rejection.

In high school, I used my female charm as I had on my father, but on a more public scale. Whereas my older brother had been class president, I arranged to get myself appointed a drum majorette for the marching band. I got a lot more public exposure than the class president did, and my picture was all over the yearbook, too.

As I moved on through adolescence, I was reasonably confident that my charm would get me what I wanted, although inside, it wasn't long before I knew that charm wasn't enough. I continued to feel rejected, angry and rebellious, now smoking and drinking my way into the "in" crowd. This was just the opposite from what my parents wanted for me and from what my brother was. I guess it was my way of punishing them both.

Anyway, that was my state when I graduated from high school in 1954, and promptly left home to entice the world to bow adoringly at my feet. But the world didn't go for it, and within four years I found myself wrung out at the end of a miserable relationship, flat on my face, begging God to help me. Don't ask me why; maybe I figured He would give me what everyone else had failed to.

All by myself, sobbing uncontrollably on the floor of my apartment on a cold, wintry January night, I called out to God. "Please, *please!* Help me, God! There's *got* to be more in life than what I've found. I'd rather be dead than hurt like this over and over again." And indeed, the thought of suicide had been stronger in recent months and was almost a comfort in my moments of despair.

As I lay there, my despair subsided, and in its place came a new, unaccustomed peace. And from that moment, my life began to change, Though I didn't know what had happened until six months later, I had undergone, of all things, a conversion! It was an inauspicious beginning to a journey that would lead me in an entirely new direction. Christ wanted to be the *center* of my life. I had always gone to church, but now

I went with a new spark of joy. I began to read the Bible whenever I could, and I knew God personally for the first time.

My parents and friends saw a difference in me. I couldn't explain it and didn't try to, but, for the first time in my life, I knew I was going in the right direction. I stopped putting such ridiculous demands on my parents' love, and I began to really love *them* and be grateful for the home and life that they had given to me. I finally became a daughter to them. Mom and I would talk for hours over a cup of tea. Many, many times we went to the retreat center in our little town, Whitinsville, for what they called "quiet days" with a beautiful Episcopalian teacher, Estelle Carver. We were blessed richly by these experiences together.

But now the news of Mom's cancer threatened to put an abrupt stop to our new relationship, and we were all hurting.

During that week in New Hampshire, she was able to talk openly about her fear of dying, her anxiety over leaving my dad with such a young son to raise, and her desire to know more of God. As she listened to Cay and Judy, she began to trust God for her own life and the life of her family. It was a tremendous relief to her to *know* that God would take care of Dad and Brian. She counseled privately with Cay and Judy, and they led her, so lovingly and gently, into facing both her life and her death in and with Jesus. Coming to grips with those facts was a deeply emotional experience for her and for me. There were times of great joy and laughing, and times of crying and weeping together.

The reality of life and death was before us continually those ten days, in a way neither of us had ever seen it. She wanted to live, but she knew that dying in Christ was even better. It was a struggle. But, in spite of the depth of emotion we were both experiencing, we found a deep, inner release from God that was unexplainable. Each day, from that time on, was a gift from God. And He extended her time with us for a whole year beyond the doctor's expectation. She died July 4, 1966.

Needless to say, our reactions to Cay and Judy were no longer mixed. Bill started inviting them to our church in Bridgeport and then to Parkminster, in Rochester, when we moved. They stayed in our home and spent evenings sitting around the living room and sharing with us about the daily reality of God, as He worked in and through the people around us. It wasn't deep, theological teaching, just the truth of how Jesus works in the most mundane things of life and uses them to help us to grow. They saw God in all the little things of life, in spilled milk and broken dishes, in blossoming trees and in thunderstorms. God was a part of everything for Cay and Judy, and that's what we loved about them.

By the time of this spring luncheon, in 1973, the Lord had raised up a Christian community at Rock Harbor. A dozen families had joined with the Andersens and Sorensens, to put into practice the simple, practical truths which Cay and Judy taught.

The luncheon was an unqualified success, as Cay and Judy shared from their lives; the 250 guests were alternately moved to laughter and to solemn reflection. And it marked only the beginning of a wonderful week of learning and growth for a great many people at Parkminster, including me.

I'm a judgmental person. I didn't like it, for example, when the women serving the luncheon that day failed to serve the head table first. And I didn't like the serving dishes they had picked to use. I wanted to look good in front of Cay and Judy, and I wanted the church to look good, and so those things and more were irritating me. But as Cay and Judy began to talk about judgments and how destructive they were, I listened. And before long, tears were rolling down my cheeks through the rest of their talk. It was as if they had been aware of all my thoughts during lunch. The more they talked, the more distressed I became.

It wasn't just the thoughts I had at this luncheon—I now saw that I was judging all the time.

I could not stop crying. Even when everyone else was laughing, I could hardly get a full smile on my face. I wasn't sure I was going to be able to make it through the luncheon. And I was embarrassed. I tried brushing my tears away as inconspicuously as possible—praying no one would notice. After all, I was the senior minister's wife and I had to keep my poise in front of 250 women! Or so I thought. Bill was arranging private counseling sessions after the luncheon, for those who wanted to talk with Cay and Judy. "Do you think I could see them first?" I whispered to him. I felt like I had to get my judgments out to Cay and Judy quickly, before I could be of any use to Bill or the church or my family. So I became the first in line for private counseling in the chapel.

The moment I walked in and saw them, I burst out crying. "I'm a mess and I really need help!"

"Here, Carol," Judy said, smiling and handing me a Kleenex. "What seems to be going on in you?"

I expected a two-hour counseling session, but in less than ten minutes it was over. "Let God continue to convict you of your judgments and show you more of your wrong attitudes at church and at home. Stop trying to relieve the pressure you're under—let it work for you." I assured them I would take their advice, but underneath I think I was miffed that they took so little time with me. They didn't seem the least bit concerned. I felt overwhelmed and shocked at what I had just learned about myself. The minister's wife of this large Presbyterian church in Rochester was full of judgments towards dozens of people in the church. What a lousy Christian I was! Why weren't they more surprised?

The mission continued. Cay and Judy talked about how difficult it was for Christians to be wrong. "Christians don't seem to understand that Christ is the only righteous one," Judy said. "When you see that you are wrong, then you see how much you need Jesus. It is your wrongness that entitles you to a Savior." I had never seen that before. After I had committed my life to God, I thought I could no longer be really wrong about anything. A good Christian was supposed to do everything right, so I kept my ugly thoughts hidden, as if they weren't even there. But invariably, the thought—or a worse one—would come back. I was living in a pretend world.

Cay and Judy told us that Jesus died for our wrongness. We did not have to work, work, work at being right, but instead we had to flee to Jesus in our wrongness. I didn't know exactly what that meant, but I wanted to find out. I was seeing my need for Jesus Christ, as I had not seen it before. When I was converted fourteen years before, I knew that I needed Christ to change my life and save me from some pretty ugly sins. But I didn't realize, until this mission, how much I needed Him every day. Left to myself, I was jealous, critical, and judgmental of everyone around me. Oh, I seldom expressed these thoughts directly, but they consumed a great deal of my time, and I knew it. And so did God.

The mission began at the noon luncheon on Monday and lasted until Thursday afternoon. Every minute was busy. Cay and Judy taught morning and evening sessions and counseled individuals each afternoon. I wanted to ask a million questions and get all kinds of personal attention, but I remembered their counsel. "Let it work for you, Carol—don't take God's pressure off yourself. " And I had felt progressively lighter and freer as the week went on. I felt God's hand on me, convicting me and then forgiving me. It was amazing! It had been a long times since I had felt the presence of God so continually in my life—all day long!

Just before they were about to leave, I had another opportunity to talk with them. "I've seen so much about myself during this week, but I don't know how to begin to change.

I see very clearly what a critical, judgmental person I am. And I've begun to see how much I have hurt the people around me with this attitude. But what do I do about it?"

"It takes time to overcome the attitudes of judgment that you have indulged in for years. But it can be done," Cay smiled. "Why don't you submit yourself to a discipline for a specific period of time. That's what we find works at the Community."

"What do you mean, what kind of discipline?"

"A self-imposed discipline not to say a critical word about anything for a certain period of time," she answered.

"Sure, I'll do that, but whom would I submit to?"

"How about Bill?" Judy asked.

"I'd be delighted!" he responded abruptly. "Frankly, I'm sick and tired of listening to all of her judgments. I'm constantly defeated by her critical attitude towards me and the children."

I winced. It was one thing for me to admit my problem; it was another to have Bill confirm it so bluntly. I pulled in, and they saw it. I hated to think anyone, including Bill, had noticed my sin. I thought I had concealed it. I didn't speak, but the hurt was written all over my face. My ugliness had not been hidden at all, and I was embarrassed by Bill's quick comments. My pretend world was crumbling fast.

"Don't be so hurt by Bill's honesty," Judy said. "You need to see that sin does affect those around you. It should make you want to change even more."

I knew she was right, but I was having a difficult time coming up over the feelings I was having. And now I was getting really angry at Bill for exposing me like that. And Judy's next suggestion only made it worse. "I think you should be under a discipline not to say a critical word to Bill for three months. And he should help you keep this discipline."

"*Three months!* Three whole months without saying one critical thing? I'll never make it!"

"By God's grace, you can, Carol, if you really want to," Cay said gently. "Pray about it and see if that's not what God would have you do. Strong habit patterns need radical steps to overcome the hold they have on our lives, because they pull us away from God."

She spoke with such compassion—like she knew exactly how difficult it would be. But she also spoke with confidence and faith that God would help it all to happen a lot easier than I could imagine at that moment.

"Stick with it, and it will begin a new work in your life," Judy said, getting out of the car, and before we knew it they were on their way back to Cape Cod, looking almost as refreshed and renewed as they had when they had arrived.

I was wiped out. I felt like I had been working ten hours a day since Monday, and there was not an ounce of strength left in me. How could I possibly begin a discipline like they had suggested? That would take more fight than I had in me. I wanted to just forget their suggestion, but Bill didn't let me. I had all kinds of reasons why I couldn't possibly go on such a discipline. "God will give you the strength you need," Bill said confidently. "I really believe He has spoken through Cay and Judy, and now you must act on what you've heard."

The first two weeks on the discipline were awful. It seemed like my whole life had been one monstrous judgment. I could hardly speak a sentence that didn't begin, "I don't like the. . ." or "Why didn't you. . ." or "Your tie doesn't. . ." My hand was over my mouth most of the time. "I'm sorry, Bill," seemed to be the only thing I could say for days. It was hard, but I was coming to see myself as I never had before. And I was grieved at what I saw. I had been tearing down my relationship with Bill and the children. And I asked God to forgive and change me—using this period of three months to start the change process.

The things that upset me—the top being left off the toothpaste, the newspaper beside the bed in the morning, the phone calls made just before dinner was served—were so trivial. But I used to badger them to death with my complaints. I think Bill and the kids had become almost deaf to me, so that, if I had ever had anything important to say, they probably couldn't have heard me. For three months I had to look for things to be grateful for, instead of poisoning the air with criticisms, morning, noon and night. And especially at meal times, when I customarily let each member of the family know just where he or she was failing around the house.

"Tim, the wastebaskets didn't get emptied again. You are so lazy and forgetful. . . Betsy, your room was a mess. When are you going to learn how to be neat?. . . Peter, if I find the Legos out of their box again, I'll get rid of them and spank you. . . The dog's dishes weren't washed, there are toys out in the yard that need to be put away. . ." On and on the litany of complaint went, meal after meal.

Yes, the children did need to hear those things every day, in order to be taught responsibility, but my attitude was terrible. There was absolutely nothing any of them could do to satisfy me. I wasn't telling them those things to help them at all; instead of constructive criticism, it was destructive.

So, for this period of time, Bill took the full responsibility to keep the children in tow with their various chores around the house. I needed Bill's help so much. And how I needed God! I was forced to pray all day, not on my knees with my eyes closed and hands folded, but just continuously talking to Him. "God, help me with what I saw this morning. And give me a grateful heart tonight at dinner." I was beginning to understand how God could be an active part of all the events of our home, no matter how small and mundane they seemed. And it was different for me to need God and Bill so much.

I had disciplined myself many times before in my life—

for a period of time—and with some sort of goal in mind. But never had I needed or desired the moment-by-moment help of anyone else, including God.

In Weight Watchers, the lecturer would say, "Before you know it, your tastes will change. You won't want to eat those foods you now love so much." To me, that meant that someday I would not have to even bother to resist; my desires would be gone, and it would all just happen without any more effort on my part. But that day never came for me. I still loved apple pie and chocolate ice cream as much as ever. The self-imposed discipline helped me to achieve my goal weight, but it didn't change my desires at all. And, whenever I cheated on my diet or gained any weight, I would just stay away from the meetings. That way, I didn't have to face my failure.

God had to be a part of any change that was going to happen in my life, if it was going to last. And for my own good, someone close to me had to be involved with imposing that discipline on me—in this case, Bill. It put me in a very safe position of not being able to do it alone.

My feeling about discipline had been that it was a form of punishment and only used to correct outward behavior. But now I saw the possibility of it being used by God to work a change deep inside of me. In fact, not only did I see that possibility; I felt it happening to me. At the beginning of the three months, I felt like I was tied up with a thick rope, not able to move without pain. That changed. Instead of feeling bound, the opposite was happening, and I was feeling free. Free from my damnable judgments and critical attitude toward my husband and children. And funny thing, I was literally falling in love anew with my family.

3

The Sand of Cape Cod

Brrrring. . . Brrrring. . . "I'm coming, just a minute!" I yelled up from the family room at the telephone ringing itself off the wall in the kitchen. Why did that phone always have to ring just when I was in the middle of loading the washer? Knowing how easily I could get involved on the phone, I shoved the load in quickly and ran upstairs.

"Hello?" I answered breathlessly.

"Carol, sorry to bother you (the phone had rung a good ten times before I had answered). I—I really need help." The voice was shaky and scared. I tried to attach a face to it. She was crying and talking at the same time and desperately trying to control the crying. "School has been out only two weeks, and I can't bear to think about the whole summer. . . I'll never make it!" And now she was sobbing in between her words. "Not only are the children home all day, but of course Bob is, too."

I had the face now; it was Lois, a very bright but insecure mother who had recently joined the church. Her husband Bob taught school in the city, and they had two young active children. I had had lunch with her not too long ago at Ruth Bailey's home.

I didn't know Lois well, but that day at lunch I had begun

to be concerned for her. She was extremely uptight about a project she had undertaken at her daughter Jenny's elementary school. Ruth and I had suggested that she make an appointment with Bill for some counseling. The last I heard, she had stopped working on the project, and her uptightness had lifted noticeably. But that was hardly the case today.

"I just can't stand the confusion around here! Bob just left with the children for the day. I suppose he hopes that will help me, but I know it will be the same when he gets home," and she started crying again. "It seemed like I just got on my feet from that whole mess at Jenny's school, and now the summer vacation is pulling me down. It's just one thing after another."

There was a long pause. "I actually considered running away—just for a few days. I have a good bike and a pup tent, and I could find a secluded place alone somewhere and try to get my head together." (I really felt like laughing, as I pictured her riding through the middle of town on her bike with a pup tent, but I knew she was serious and this was not the time to laugh.) "The next thing I thought about doing was going to the liquor store and buying a bottle of something and getting drunk." (I was pretty sure she didn't drink, so this, too, made me want to laugh.) "But," she went on, "I knew that when I sobered up, I still would have to face my family and myself."

Another long pause. I slipped into a comfortable chair in the living room, realizing this was going to be a long telephone call. Thank God for 10-foot-long telephone cords!

"My third choice was to call you for help. Can you, will you, help me?"

"Of course, Lois," I said, "I'm not sure how, but I will if I can." And as she went on, sounding somewhat relieved, I suddenly became aware of what I was getting into. Why didn't she call Bill? He's the trained counselor, not me! I tried to pray as she talked, but my own questions kept interrupting my prayers. *I hope she's not suicidal. Lord, what in the world can I do for her?*

She just went on expressing the hopeless state of confusion she felt. "Is there any way out?" she finally asked with a desperate edge to her voice.

Now the pause was on my end of the telephone line; I had no idea what to say to her. The words that finally came out floored me. "Lois, I think I'm supposed to come over today, but not to talk to you. And I think I'm supposed to bring someone with me. And the three of us are supposed to clean your house." *What in the world had I said?* I had never been in Lois' house and had no idea whether it needed cleaning, and furthermore, what business was it of mine whether or not it did need cleaning? The thought had just popped into my head and out of my mouth.

She burst out laughing. And I felt like a jerk. "You're going to come over and help me clean my house? What makes you think I need help around the house?"

I didn't even attempt to answer that. "Lois, that's what I think I'm supposed to do to help you," I said, getting a little irritated. "Do you want my help or not?"

She laughed some more. Again, I felt stupid for even offering to do such a thing, and I wished now I could just hang up the phone. "Sure, I'd love to have you come over and clean for me." By this time, I didn't want to go, but I still had the feeling that that was what God wanted.

"Okay, I'll be over as soon as I can." I stood there, staring at the phone, half wishing that I had never answered it. *Now what was I going to do? God, help me.* I could think of a dozen things I needed to do around my own house. I had a choice at that moment, standing there, between going to Lois' or forgetting the whole thing. Everything in me wanted to call her back and tell her to go see Bill and get the real help she

29

needed. But when I picked up the phone, I dialed Helene, my reliable babysitter, instead. I explained that I needed her help for a special project and wondered if she would be willing. "Sure, Mrs. Showalter, I wasn't busy at all—I'd be glad to help." Boy, was I grateful. There was no way I wanted to go alone to a strange house and clean with an emotional woman I hardly knew.

So off we went. More questions harassed me on the drive over. What if her husband comes back? Will he be angry, finding me in their house, cleaning? What if she is too upset to clean? Maybe I've insulted her with my offer? How could I have been so presumptuous!

We pulled into her driveway, or at least what I hoped was her driveway. "Helene, would you look in my pocketbook and see if I jotted down the house number?" She was rustling through some papers, when I saw Lois at the front door. "Never mind, there's Lois now."

Lois was trying to greet us with a smile, but it was a hurt, scared smile. "Come on in. The house is a mess, and I'm a mess, too. But you already know that, or you wouldn't be here," she said, with a nervous laugh. For a moment the three of us just stood there in the darkened living room, tense and uncomfortable.

The draperies were closed, making the house appear very dark and dreary. There were toys scattered around the floor but certainly nothing unusually out of order. Beyond the living room, I could see a dining area and the kitchen. Although it was nearly eleven o'clock, the breakfast dishes were waiting to be loaded into the dishwasher, and the cereal boxes were still out on the table. What were we supposed to do now?

There didn't seem to be a nice, smooth way to get into this, so I just jumped in. "Helene, why don't you go out to the kitchen and start clearing up the counters and doing the dishes."

"Sure," she answered, and off she went. I had explained to her in the car, as best I could, what I thought we would be doing, and she thought it was a great idea to help someone out like this. Her enthusiasm helped me, since I had come to think that it was not such a good idea!

"Lois, if you'll get the vacuum out and some dust cloths and furniture polish, I'll start in right here," I said, pointing to the living room area. "How about laundry? Are you all caught up?" I asked.

Another outburst of laughter. It seemed her laughing was almost as spontaneous as her crying. "Caught up? There are at least three loads downstairs to wash and several more to fold and put away."

"Okay, why don't you make that your project for a few hours."

I noticed a large stereo console at the other end of the living room, and the thought came to me to suggest we listen to some good Christian music, so I did. Lois was delighted. I found out she loved music and, in fact, wanted to take piano lessons as soon as she could find time. Before going off to the laundry room, she put on a record of favorite hymns.

The first thing I did was to pull back the draperies. Then I opened the front door and a couple of windows to let in the warm July air. The darkness lifted immediately, and the music encouraged us in our tasks.

I had to leave at noon, but Helene volunteered to carry on after lunch, if I would come back for her later in the afternoon.

When I returned, about three o'clock, Bob and the children were home, and they were all smiles. Lois' mood was totally different. "I feel so much better!" she called out to me in the driveway, loud enough for the neighbors to hear, I feared.

"I don't know how on earth cleaning the house could make such a difference—it usually works just the opposite way on me and makes me more depressed," she said, walking over towards me. "I know it helped me to have you and Helene here. Thanks a million."

"It did seem like a pretty strange answer to your upset and tears," I laughed, "but it worked, and we can thank God for that."

Helene talked all the way home about what fun she had working with Lois, "And guess what?" she exclaimed, "she wants me to come back two or three mornings for the next few weeks, and she'll pay me! Which is great, because I need to save some money for the church's senior high retreat in September."

I shook my head in wonder at how it had all worked out. Bill was astounded, when I told him about it that evening. "Honey," he chuckled, "you've just broken every rule in counseling. Here I am, about to get my doctorate in the subject, and never have I heard or read anywhere that the answer to a woman's depression is for the counselor to run over and clean her house." He laughed. "And since when do ministers' wives offer cleaning services as part of their jobs?" And now we both laughed.

"I don't know much about counseling, but you have to admit it worked. And if housecleaning did the trick, maybe it *should* be in one of your text books!"

We laughed some more, but inside we both felt very grateful to God. Bill had counseled Lois in the past, and he felt it was a real miracle that her depression had lifted so quickly.

Several weeks later, Lois called again early one morning. She wasn't the same woman. "Oh, I still have all those problems I mentioned to you that day on the phone, but I feel one-hundred-percent better about them all. I know God is going to see me through. I don't feel desperate or hopeless any more." And there was hope in her voice, and trust—so different from that time a few weeks earlier. We decided to get together and sit down and work out a daily plan for her housework and her needs with the children. It was clear to both of us that when things were confused around the house, it had affected her emotionally. As long as Bob and the children had been at school, it imposed a certain schedule in their household. But when school was out, that schedule had evaporated. So we both agreed she needed her own schedule, and she asked me to help her make one.

Naturally, a summer schedule would be different from one for school days. The children could stay up a little later, and Bob and she could sleep in a little in the mornings. But lunch time was set at quarter past twelve, instead of everyone just eating when they got hungry. It had turned out in the past that with no time set for lunch, it ran from 11:30, when little Andy felt hungry, to 1:15, when Bob got around to eating, thus dragging it out far too long for Lois. We also decided on specific times for the two other meals, and then we loosely divided the day into housework chores in the morning and kids' activities and shopping in the afternoon.

Lois was genuinely excited about the prospect of running the house in the summer with some sort of organization. And Bob, too, was well pleased, responding to it enthusiastically and supporting Lois in implementing it right away.

As they left church the following Sunday, Bob waited outside of the door for a few minutes to speak to us. "Things are so different around our house these past few weeks, you wouldn't believe it! And we are all feeling a lot better. I really appreciate all you've done." His eyes filled, as he put his hand out to shake hands with Bill. My eyes filled, too, and I reached out and gave him a big hug.

"Just think, Dad, only eight more days, and then no more telephone calls for a whole month!" Those were the words of our son Tim, as August approached. Tomorrow it would be "just think, Dad, only seven more days. . ." August—Bill's vacation month—was just around the corner, and soon we'd be off to Cape Cod, our favorite spot.

Our first Cape Cod vacation had been in the early 1960's, when the grandfather of a girl in our church in Bridgeport gave us the keys to his cottage for a month. We loved it and had a glorious time, but never felt we could afford to go back. Instead, we tried various attempts at vacationing, none of which was very acceptable; Christian camps, where the cost was low and the spiritual activity high; and then we tried "visit-the-family," which was never very relaxing. So we kept searching, not quite satisfied with our vacations, hoping someday to find the perfect spot. It was so important to get away from the phone and appointments and just relax, but at the same time we also knew that we needed some spiritual intake during that month, or the busy fall schedule would overwhelm us.

Then it had happened. In addition to Rock Harbor Manor, the guest house which Bill and Cay Andersen owned in Orleans on Cape Cod, they had a small cottage which they rented out during the summer. It sounded just like what we were looking for—two bedrooms, a kitchen, bath, and front room snuggled in a quiet grove of locust trees behind the guest house, only a five-minute walk to the beach. We had rented it, sight unseen, for the month of August, 1966. Our family loved it. And there was lots of Christian fellowship to be had. Twice a week, on Monday and Thursday evenings, in the living room of the guest house, there was a time of sharing and teaching, open to anyone who wanted to come. There we met people from all over New England as well as from the Cape—vacationers who, like us, wanted more than just a vacation.

We looked forward to those informal gatherings in such gracious surroundings. Cay and Judy would sit on a sofa, and I had never seen two people who could share as easily as they. Their words blended together as if only one person were speaking. One would pause and the other would begin, and the unbroken continuity of their thoughts was amazing. And not only did their words blend beautifully, and their personalities, but Cay's blond hair and light complexion complemented Judy's dark hair and eyes. Even the colors in their dresses were compatible, never drawing attention to themselves, but each deferring to the other. It was a joy and privilege to sit and listen and watch these two women, whom God had obviously set apart for a special call in life.

Sometimes there would be as many as forty people sitting in the spacious living room, including six or seven ministers and their wives. As Cay and Judy shared, Bill from time to time would leaf through his Bible for the pertinent Scripture reference, but I just sat, captivated by the life of Christ I saw and sensed coming through them. And when the meeting was over, no one wanted to leave. It was fun just standing around, talking to one another and getting acquainted.

After a while, many of us regulars began to get together at other times during the week. An Episcopal priest, Father Arthur Lane, of St. Paul's in Darien, Connecticut, had a beautiful waterfront cottage in Harwichport, to which he and his wife would invite us for a day of picnicking and swimming. Monday and Thursday nights soon became for us, times to meet with friends as well as to learn more about the down-to-earth practicalities of daily living in Christ.

We returned to that cottage at Rock Harbor the next summer, and in fact for the next four summers. Change, however, was inevitable around the quiet guest house and cottage. The Christian community that was rapidly growing up there became officially incorporated on June 19, 1970.

I'll never forget what happened the first Sunday morning we were there that summer. Bill had decided to sleep out on the porch in a sleeping bag to fully enjoy the warm summer evening. About eight-thirty in the morning, half-awake, I heard the strangest thumping around on the porch. I jumped up and could hardly believe my eyes! Bill was trying to make his way into the living room—still in the sleeping bag ! He was standing upright and holding it up, or trying to hold it up, with one hand, while giving me some kind of frantic signal with the other. His finger was up over his lips and then pointed outside.

"There's church going on out there in the locust grove," he whispered. "Art has his surplice on and is conducting a communion service."

I looked out the living room window, my eyes widening. Sure enough, there was Father Lane, standing behind a small table that was serving as an altar. He had a long white robe on and was reading from the prayer book. The wind was lifting the ends of the white cloth that covered the table, and the candles were flickering. There were four neat rows of folding chairs that had not been there when we went to bed. And standing in front of them were some guests and the thirty or so people who had become a part of the Community of Jesus. They were more than just a group of people buying houses in the area—they were obviously already a family, sharing their faith in God.

Bill and I had recently talked about the changes we saw happening around the little cottage. The locust grove seemed to have become a center of activity almost daily, with volleyball games and croquet and a mid-afternoon coffee hour. We had mixed emotions—happiness for these families who seemed to have a very special relationship with one another—but sadness too, that we were losing our quiet, secluded hideaway.

I think we both knew, although neither of us said anything, that when we turned in our key that Labor Day, we would not be renting the cottage again. There was sadness deep inside me when, as we started up the old Dodge, the kids called out, "Goodbye, cottage, until next year." I wondered where we would be next August.

Where we would be, it turned out, was as far in the opposite direction as possible. The following summer, 1971, we loaded the new family station wagon to the gunwales and headed west. Horses, mountains, camping—we spent most of our month immersed in a completely different kind of a vacation. And it was a good trip, but though we seldom mentioned it, we found ourselves missing the fellowship at the Community. It seemed like we had a lot more than just the sand in our shoes from the Cape; we had a deep love in our heart for our summer friends. It seemed that the Cape had become far more special to us than we had realized.

After nearly three weeks of the west we found ourselves on our way home, about 10 days sooner than we planned. And coincidently we found that we had just enough time left in our vacation month to take a fast trip to the Cape. Our station wagon went right by the Rochester exits and on towards the Mass pike. There were no complaints from the family and although there were few words spoken between Bill and me there was a mutual agreement that we were now headed in the right direction.

As we drove over the Sagamore Bridge on to the Cape, we both sensed a distinct feeling of coming home. I think it was then that we finally accepted what our hearts had known for some time—that Cape Cod had become far more than a vacation spot to us. The next summer we rented a cottage a few minutes from the Community, and just before we went back to Rochester we made a major commitment. We bought a piece of land, with the dream of building a cottage of our own as soon as possible.

4

3D

August of '73 was unusually warm, and I was delighted to be able to have dinner out on the patio of our little rented cottage. The sun was setting, the mosquitoes were bearable, and the air was delightful. Hot plates, cut celery, plenty of ice in the iced tea, everything was ready, and Peter and Edith Marshall, friends of ours, were due in a few minutes. My last-minute check-list continued—the bread cups were out of the oven, crisp and browned perfectly, and would soon be filled with a shrimp-cheese Newburg. The garden asparagus was washed and ready for cooking. The smell of fresh-baked blueberry buckle filled the cottage with a most inviting aroma.

I stopped for a moment and listened to the evening. Cape Cod was so inundated with visitors that you could almost hear the hum of activity. In two weeks, the day after Labor Day, the Cape would be silent and peaceful, but right now, the tourist season was at its peak. I took a last look at the table and went to get out of my apron. They would be coming any minute. Peter and Edith were leaving shortly, to get away on a canoe trip to Maine with a group from church, and we wanted to touch base with them before they left.

The doorbell rang around seven, and that was the last time I looked at the clock. Once again, time seemed to fly by, and the dinner tasted good outside by candlelight. Before I knew it, it was time for dessert. I brought out the warm blueberry buckle, piled high with whipped cream and sprinkled with fresh blueberries. Serving the others and then putting an ample portion down at my own place, I remarked lightly, "Oh well, I'll start my diet again tomorrow."

Edith picked up on that comment and said, "Do you remember that group I told you about which met during February and March at church?"

I thought for a moment. "I do remember something about a group that you started, to help people with different problems, including weight. Is that the one you mean?"

"That's the one," she said. "You know, it turned out to be a real blessing for a lot of people, including me."

It was quite a story to hear. She shared how a group of people sat around a big maple table at the home of some close friends. Peter and Edith were frustrated with the needs of the people in their church. They seemed to have so many practical problems, like finances and housework and dieting and drinking and even nail-biting! Peter knew how to·preach and his faith was exuberant but getting faith down to the· practical, nitty-gritty problems facing these Cape Cod families wasn't working.

After listening to all the different problems of the church people, Cay Andersen smiled and said, "Well, it sounds to me like all the problems you have been talking about come down to diet, discipline, and discipleship—3 big D's!" She laughed and her eyes twinkled with the simple answer God gave her to a very complex problem.

Everyone around the table responded enthusiastically, and the decision was made to start a support-group program that would be Christ-centered. It would deal with dieting, drinking, finances, and any other areas that would respond to self-discipline.

Now Peter picked up the narrative, shifting his six foot-four frame and continuing with a grin. "God took charge from there on," he explained. "I announced the meeting the next Sunday and made it pretty clear that certain unnamed members had better seriously consider this group for the help they needed." He chuckled. "Before we knew it, more than fifty people were ready for a six week program."

Peter and Edith felt that they were not supposed to lead the group themselves, so they turned to the Community of Jesus, asking for some leadership. Cay and Judy encouraged two ministers' wives to go over to East Dennis—Jane Witter, who had recently shed more than fifty pounds herself, and Lenny Lane, who had studied nutrition.

"It went so well," said Edith, "that at the end of the six weeks we had agreed upon, Lenny and Jane offered to continue a group at the Community for any who were interested in going on. From all reports, we heard everyone was very happy with the results. I lost my ten pounds in the six weeks, so I was more than satisfied." She paused, then remembered something.

"Oh! Guess what we named the group?" Edith laughed. "3D—for Diet, Discipline and Discipleship."

For no reason, just then into my mind popped the image of that red 'smile' face in the East Hall at church. Now what did that have to do with—could *this* be God's answer?

Suddenly I had a million questions to ask. But it was late, and it would have been wrong to hold our guests any longer. As they were leaving, I said, "Edith, when we get back to Rochester, and you get back from Maine, I'd like to give you a call to get some more details about the 3D thing." That was all that was said, but that night I could not get to sleep. The little that Peter and Edith had shared had started an avalanche of thoughts in my head. It was like being given just one lick of a mocha almond ice-cream cone—I wanted much more!

For the remainder of our vacation, I could hardly get my mind off 3D. Bill and I were sitting on the beach one afternoon, watching the children swim, when for the umpteenth time, I started wondering who back home might be interested in such a group. And the list of questions I wanted to ask Edith grew longer and longer. But Edith was off in Maine canoeing, so I pestered Bill instead.

"Bill?"

"Mm?" he said, absorbed in *Time* magazine.

"Do you think Dorcas might be interested, hon?"

"Interested in what?" he murmured, not looking up.

"Interested in a 3D group back at church."

"Maybe."

"I bet Margaret and Dee would be, because of their weight problem, don't you?"

"Well," he replied, throwing me a quick glance, "I suppose you won't know till you get home and ask them, right?" And he turned back to *Time*.

I knew all he wanted was to read in peace, but it didn't seem fair that he should be so peaceful when I was anything but. "Hon, Edith said she was able to lose ten pounds during the six weeks. . . I haven't lost ten pounds in the last year, trying by myself!"

No answer, not even a grunt.

"I'll bet Norma would love to be involved in a Christian weight group—and Mary Jane is anxious to take off the weight she gained since Kirk was born. That's already five others besides me for a group, and I'll bet Lois would join, too."

No answer—then "Mmf," as I poked him in the side.

"Hey, take it easy!" he chuckled, grabbing my wrist. "Sounds to me like that group has already started, but you haven't talked to one person yet. What's more, there's no way you can talk to anyone, until we get back to Rochester. So why don't you put this whole 3D thing out of your mind and enjoy the last of our vacation. Remember, it will be a whole year before we can get back here." And he put the magazine over his eyes and settled himself for a snooze.

Bill was right, of course. It was typical of me to get so wrapped up in something that I forgot everything else. I needed to be thinking about my family and our vacation and not some new program. There would be lots of time for that after Labor Day.

So I did the best I could. I stopped talking about it—but it was more than I could do to stop thinking about it.

Before we knew it, Labor Day had arrived. And that meant that we would leave at five the next morning, for our long journey home. What a blessing that one extra day after the holidays was! The traveling was much easier with most of the vacationers already off the Cape and back home.

We tucked boxes and bags into every conceivable corner of the station wagon, and the suitcases were strapped onto the luggage rack on the roof. We locked the cottage door, and off we went. It was one of those perfect driving days—sunny, but breezy too, with fluffy white clouds scudding across the sky. As soon as we passed the Albany exits on the thruway, we began to get anxious for the sight and sound of Rochester. For some reason, Albany and east seemed to be the Cape Cod side of the trip, and everything west of Albany meant we were nearing home. It was funny how certain places had become landmarks on our many trips to and from Cape Cod—the bridge to the mainland, our breakfast stop at the Friendly's in Auburn, the two Albany exits, the cheap gas and ice cream stop in Herkimer, and then Rochester.

The children couldn't wait to call their friends the minute we got in the door, and Bill couldn't wait to get his mail from the office. I couldn't wait to get the suitcases emptied and get settled in our own rooms and know we'd be sleeping in our very own beds. And once all the baths and shampoos were over, and the new school clothes laid out on the beds, and prayers said on that Tuesday night, we knew vacation was far behind us.

The buzz around Parkminster was always fantastic in September. It was exhilarating to go over and watch all the activity—the preschool teachers and aides scrubbing and cleaning, the Sunday School staff getting the nursery and the other classrooms ready, and various people painting and cleaning around the church. Choir rehearsals and youth groups would be starting the first Wednesday in September, and the leaders were busy getting music and materials ready. The moment the kids were off to school Wednesday morning, I put on my jacket and took the familiar walk across the yard to the church.

I recognized Jean Leyland's car in the parking lot. Jean was the program chairman for the women's association and one of the most active women in our church; she would be the perfect one to try out 3D on!

And just then, as if on cue, she came hurrying out. "Hi, Carol, welcome home!" she said, pausing on her way to her car. "Hope you had a good restful vacation on Cape Cod."

"We did! We enjoyed every minute, as usual."

I could see she was in a hurry, but I didn't want to let her go until I at least mentioned 3D. "Jean, I learned about the most exciting group that met at Peter Marshall's church last winter and at the Community of Jesus. It really sounds like just what we need around —"

"I'd love to hear about it," she said, opening the door of her car. "Maybe we can get together after the fall luncheon."

After the fall luncheon! My heart sank. That meant October! "I guess I thought it was something we could maybe start soon, like next week. . . and I —"

"Oh, Carol," she said, trying to say it kindly, but revealing the pressure she was under, "there's no way I can even think about another program until next spring! And I still have to find committee chairmen for several openings that have come up over the summer months."

From my own term as program chairman, I should have appreciated all the pressure she was under, but I didn't appreciate anything but 3D. "It's called a diet, discipline and discipleship group," I went on hurriedly, "and, in a sense, it is a Christ-oriented counterpart of Weight Watchers. The Bible is used, and prayer is a basic tool to help women get more disciplined in—"

"Carol, please forgive me, but I've got to run. I'm late for a luncheon committee meeting. It's great to have you back again." And she waved, as she got in her car and closed the door.

Standing there and watching her back out and pull away, I waved, but inside I felt like crying. I tried to tell myself how busy she was, and how unfair it had been of me to grab her and spring 3D on her. But I was also thinking that she had such a good figure and no problem or any lack of self-discipline, so of course she wouldn't be interested.

I tried also to remind myself, walking into the church, that if this was indeed God's answer, it would somehow all work out. But not even the smell of fresh paint or the happy bustle of activity could lift my spirits. I started wandering toward the preschool activity. Then, I heard my name called.

"Carol? Well, Carol! Welcome home!" It was Dorcas, the wife of our assistant minister. "I saw you talking to Jean outside. Did she tell you that they've sold over a hundred tickets already for the luncheon, and it's still three weeks away?"

"Say, that's great!" I said feebly, "She certainly is busy." I realized with chagrin that I had never even asked Jean about how the luncheon was coming.

"For a supposedly quiet month," Dorcas went on, "August has been absolutely incredible around here. I hope it was quieter for you all at the Cape."

"We did see Peter and Edith a few times and had a great time visiting the Community of Jesus. There are more than eighty resident members there now, and all keeping busy from the look of things. They've got a new chapel—you wouldn't recognize the place. But I guess the most exciting thing I heard was about a new support group."

"Oh, you mean their Upper Room Fellowship?"

"No," I said, happy that I could surprise her, "a group called 3D—diet, discipline and discipleship."

"Ugh, diet! Don't even mention that word to me—please! I joined Weight Watchers and quit again, just in the month you've been away," she laughed. "I think I'm going to get a pin for being the person who has joined and quit the most in one year." I managed a weak smile. It was plain to see she was not the least bit interested in any diet group—Christian or otherwise. I didn't say any more, but inside I had the feeling that walls were caving in. I felt so down and rejected by both Jean's and Dorcas's reaction. . . Had I really heard God?

5

The Fat, the Sleepy, and the Sloppy

September began to slip away, day by day. I didn't bring up the subject of 3D again to anyone. In my hurt and rejection I decided that dieting and discipline were just not important enough to hassle about. And little by little the bathroom scale went up, as I enjoyed french fries, toll house cookies and ice cream cones whenever I could sneak them in. I was eating and enjoying it, and to heck with every thought of dieting!

One night after dinner, I suggested the whole family go out for dessert. Bill raised his eyebrows and said, "Hey, how come all these desserts and treats lately? I thought you were all gung-ho on this diet thing after we got home from the Cape." He paused. "Whatever happened to that 3D idea?"

"No one was interested," I muttered, getting up from the table to clear the dishes and hopefully end the discussion.

"What do you mean, no interest? You had enough excitement and interest on Cape Cod for ten people. And, when you get something in your head, you take off and get it together. Now come back here and sit down, and let's get to the bottom of this. What's the real problem?"

I told him how I felt, and that Jean was right; we already did have so much going on at church—"and there really isn't any time to start a new program around here. Maybe next year—"

"Carol," Bill cut me off, "I think you're being vindictive about the whole 3D thing, because Jean and Dorcas didn't buy your idea immediately. You've never really sought God's will on this. All you've done is withdraw."

He was right. I had not worked through the thing at all, just shelved the whole idea. And soothed my hurt by doing just the absolute opposite of dieting—eating anything and everything I wanted.

"It seems to me," he continued, "that you named six or seven others who you were sure would be interested. So why don't you talk to them and a few others about it?" And most important, we both agreed to pray seriously about it. If the idea was from God, Bill concluded, He would surely let us know soon.

"Anyone home?" called a voice outside our side door.

"Sure," I called out, "come on in."

In walked Lois, bright, cheerful and excited.

"I just wanted to stop by and tell you how well the summer went!" She was beaming. "It's been the best summer we've ever had! That schedule you worked out with me in July was a gift from God to me and my family."

She waited for me to respond. For a minute I couldn't remember what she was talking about, and then it dawned on me. "Oh, I'd almost forgotten about that. But I'll never forget that fun day we had cleaning!"

I was frankly amazed at her excitement and freedom. She really was different. We sat and talked and then looked over her schedule. And it looked great—beautifully organized.

"Carol, I wonder. . . well, would you mind if I checked

in with you on a regular basis, just to keep things going in the right direction?"

"Sure, as long as you don't expect me to come and clean every week," I laughed. It was a joy seeing Lois so free—so absolutely different from that encounter in July.

The next day, I had another surprise visitor. "Your husband felt I ought to come over and tell you what I just told him," Norma started. "As you know, I've lost a great deal of weight since the beginning of the year, and now I've even started lecturing in the Diet Workshop group I belong to."

"I didn't know that you were lecturing, Norma; that's great!"

"Well, I'm not sure it's so great. The reason I was able to lose the weight had more to do with my new faith in God than the diet program itself; and that really makes it hard, because I have to sell a diet program—and not talk about God at all."

I just shook my head.

"Bill tells me you are thinking about starting a diet group based on Christian principles," she continued. "I think it sounds tremendous! I'd love to be a part of it, if possible."

I must have had a surprised look on my face. "Thanks, Norma. I did think about that very seriously and then kind of dropped the idea. But it's beginning to seem more possible now."

We talked awhile, and I assured her I would get in touch with her when the plans became more concrete.

And in a few hours, I had a third unexpected visitor. Ruth Bailey walked in, nervously stopping at the top step before coming in the kitchen. "I'm sorry to just drop in this way, but Bill said he thought it would be good if I came over and talked to you. . ." Then she burst out crying. Ruth was an attractive woman, with light brown hair and soft facial features. As she spoke, her voice was almost mousey-quiet and squeaky—and because of the tears, I could hardly understand her.

"Come in the living room, Ruth, and sit down," I said, putting my arm around her shoulder. Our living room had two love-seats; she sat on one, and I sat opposite her on the other. For a few minutes she cried, and I sat there, praying silently. Her crying was coming from so deep inside, it made me hurt. I felt helpless sitting there, but I knew it was good for her just to cry, no matter how uncomfortable we both were.

"I find it really hard to talk to anyone, Carol. . . especially about my personal life. I'm a person who doesn't let people get too close to me, and I don't get too close to them." Her voice was very shaky and the crying continued in between pauses.

"All I want to do lately is sleep, sleep, sleep. The minute Dan leaves for work and the children go to school, I go back to bed and sleep half the morning away. Then, believe it or not, I go back to bed after lunch and sleep half the afternoon. I just don't want to be with anyone or do anything." She started crying hard again. "The minute people begin to get close to me, I pull away."

"What can I do to help, Ruth?" I asked.

"I don't know. . . I don't know if anyone can help me. I'm running from my responsibilities, and I'm running from my friends, and I'm running from God. I have such a good husband in Dan and three children and a beautiful home— so much to be thankful for. But I'm so unhappy with myself!" And she obviously hated herself for being so out of control of her emotions.

"Ruth, I want to help you. And for heaven's sake, don't feel embarrassed about crying."

The Baileys were newcomers to the church. She had always been friendly to me and an enjoyable person to be around. I remembered the lovely lunch she had had, the day I had gotten to know Lois. Ruth had been the perfect hostess, making us feel right at home, and her home was beautiful and decorated with taste. Like Lois, Ruth was a teacher and did substitute work at the same school. She had been concerned about the project Lois had taken on at school and how involved it had become. I remember having the distinct feeling that Ruth really cared about Lois and me. I had never dreamed she was so unhappy inside.

But thinking about Lois reminded me of the good results she had had with a daily schedule. Maybe. . .

"Ruth, ah, have you ever tried to specifically plan your day, hour by hour?" I asked sheepishly.

"You mean some sort of a daily schedule?"

I was surprised she even had any idea what I was talking about. "Yes, that's exactly what I mean. If you planned your day with certain things at specific times, you might be less tempted to go back to bed."

"Lois was telling me how much she had been helped by her new schedule," Ruth remarked. "And I can see a big change in her attitude and feelings about her house and family."

I couldn't help but wonder as Ruth talked, how a schedule would work out for her. She was not needy as far as her housework was concerned. She seemed to be able to keep a beautiful house and still have time for creativity—like flower arranging and needlepoint and things that added special touches to her home. But as she talked, her needs became more apparent.

"I started making draperies and a bedspread for our bedroom two years ago, and they're not finished yet. And I have several other projects started, but not finished. I'd also like to get to know some women from church better, and I thought it would be fun to have a few small luncheons—I love to cook and entertain. But if I don't break this habit of running off to sleep every chance I get, none of those things can get done." She seemed to relax as we talked. Her eyes were puffy, red, and swollen from crying, but she was also at ease.

We just sat and talked for quite a while about a lot of different things. I found out that her husband was an engineer for the telephone company, and that they had been involved in a Methodist church before coming to Parkminster. Ruth started coming to the Wednesday morning Bible study with a neighbor, and loved it. Then she brought Dan a few times to hear guest speakers—and gradually she found herself spending more time at Parkminster than at her own church. Soon the whole family had joined in. By the time she got up to leave, I felt a real closeness to her—the very thing she had said she would not allow people to feel. It wasn't planned; it just happened. The sharing had broken down a self-constructed barrier.

"I'm sure I look awful, but I feel better," she said as she was getting ready to leave. "Thanks a lot—I'll need help to set up my schedule. Can we get together to work on it soon?" Schedule? I had already forgotten about working out her schedule. She went on, "Will it be all right if I call or stop in before the weekend? I want to start a new way of living Monday morning," she said with a big smile.

"Sure, Ruth," I said, wondering when I was going to get the time on my own schedule to work on someone else's. I had Lois checking in with me and now Ruth—who would be next?

I had mixed emotions when she drove out of the driveway. I knew it had been hard for her to come and share her need, and she was definitely being hurt by this bondage to sleep, but where would I find time? I decided I shouldn't get worried about it. God would have to stretch my days, that was all there was to it.

That night at supper Bill asked how my day had gone. I laughed and said, "Not on schedule, that's for sure." Then I told him about my morning visitors.

"Sounds to me like God is answering our prayers about whether there should be a diet, discipline and discipleship group here," he laughed, "He sure seems to be making it obvious."

"Well, let's quickly tell the Lord I'm willing, before I have ten more women coming one by one, asking to be put on schedules."

That very night I called Lois, Ruth and Norma and shared the 3D idea with them. They thought it sounded tremendous and could think of several other women who would be interested in a group like this. So we set up a meeting time—the next Tuesday night at eight o'clock in the church lounge.

Tuesday night arrived—and so did ten women! Lois was the most enthusiastic of them all, with Ruth second. It was a funny group of people, some of us having never been together before.

I had invited Dee to come. She was a very heavy woman, a Catholic, who had called me on the phone one afternoon, in reference to something I had written in my column in the local paper. I had talked with her several times since then and knew her weight problem was a big one. She needed help and was delighted that I had asked her to our meeting, even though she didn't know anyone there but me.

Then Lois had asked Margaret, who was in choir with her, and Mary Jane if they'd be interested. They were; both were over 200 pounds. Mary Jane had lost a lot of weight a few years back, but then gained it back again during a pregnancy.

The heavier women were obviously wondering why in the world Jo Mancini and Beverly Evans were in the room. Neither of them weighed more than 120 pounds. I had asked them to come, not because they needed a diet group, but because I felt they could help us get some direction. They were both very active in Christian groups in the community with their husbands and seemed to lead very disciplined lives.

Then there was Norma, looking great from her dieting.

Helen McClurg came too. She had been in the Weight Watchers' group Dorcas and I had been part of, and like us, she had dropped out. We invited her to try 3D with some other "flunkies". And Dorcas reluctantly agreed to come too.

There was an uncomfortable silence in the room. Lois was busily introducing people to each other and still carrying the only real enthusiasm in the group. Dee seemed to be happy to meet these Protestant women. I knew I had to get the meeting started, even though I didn't have the slightest idea what we were going to do. The atmosphere was tense, the minute the talking stopped; I was scared.

"I guess I should start off." I shared my ups and downs and ins and outs with this whole 3D idea, wanting it very desperately because of my own weight problem, and yet not willing to step out on faith to begin. "I'm ready now, with God's help, to see just what He has for us. Certainly, if the secular world can offer so much help to the over-indulger, God's got to have an even better answer. More and more I am seeing, and I think others are too, that our lives are totally undisciplined."

At this point, Lois jumped in. "This summer Carol helped me get myself on a daily schedule, with specific times to clean each room in my house, do my laundry and even play the piano and hike with the kids. We took a totally disorganized life, re-arranged things with God's help, and it has literally changed my life in less than two months." She was radiant, sharing the blessings of the summer with the group.

Mary Jane talked about how defeated she was, having gained all her weight back during her pregnancy. "I need help," she said rather desperately. She was a very attractive gal in her late twenties, but her weight was an obvious burden to her.

Norma spoke of her frustration with not being able to talk about God in her lectures at the diet group.

Jo and Beverly, the two who I thought would be able to guide us, confessed a lack of self-discipline in many areas of their lives. "Just because I'm not heavy doesn't mean I'm a disciplined person," Jo said. "I need help in a lot of ways." Beverly wholeheartedly concurred, and Ruth Bailey openly shared her struggle with sleeping too much.

"Well," I announced, "here we are: the fat, the sleepy, and the sloppy, without a choice between us!" And we all roared with laughter. The tension in the air had pretty well vanished. We all agreed that we needed God's help and each other's help, and so we decided to meet every Tuesday night at eight, and just see what would happen.

The talking stopped, and someone suggested we pray before we leave. Spontaneously we stood up and joined hands in a circle. A spirit of quietness came over the room. An hour or so before, we had hardly known one another, but now, through sharing, we were becoming closer, God had been in our midst, and we all knew it.

6

Two Hearts are Better than One

"Where in the world have you been?" asked Bill drowsily, squinting at the clock. "Is that twenty minutes of twelve?"

I wished I hadn't bothered to turn on the light to get ready for bed. "I've been at the 3D meeting over at church," I replied, on my way to the bathroom.

"Four hours at a 3D meeting? That doesn't sound very much like discipline to me!"

Shutting the bathroom door a little more forcefully than I'd intended, I began to rationalize why our fourth meeting had gone so late. Down inside, I was more upset about it than he was. But instead of telling him about my frustrations and getting it off my chest, I gave in to hurt feelings again and defended myself, when I returned to the bedroom. "It was a bad week for all of us in the group, and we talked quite a bit about the problems we were having."

Bill didn't answer; he must have fallen back asleep. I reached over to shut off the lamp, somewhat relieved that he was sleeping but also somewhat angry. After all, hadn't I often waited up for him when he came home late from church meetings? But the one night *I'm* late and really need to talk to him, he's asleep and only wakes up long enough to tell me I was wrong to be late! I punched my pillow, then scolded myself for being childish, but, as usual when I was in one of those moods, I ignored my own better judgment. Just then, almost as if he had heard my thoughts, Bill rolled over and grumbled, "Ten women should not be alone in the church so late at night, especially when they still have to drive home." And he rolled back over.

"I never thought of that," I replied in a small voice, but there was no answer. Something else I never thought of was that the reasons I waited up for Bill were pretty selfish—usually I wanted to talk to him—and it didn't have a lot to do with my caring about him.

At that point I should have given the whole thing over to the Lord to resolve when and how He saw fit, and gone to sleep. Instead, I tossed and turned, thinking and churning it all around.

The group had been pretty good the first two weeks, even though we didn't seem to have much overall direction. The trouble was, we didn't know how to help each other, and we stopped short of saying what really needed to be said. For instance, I had felt that I should say something to Dee tonight about her three-pound gain, but how could I? I knew she was lonely and down because Sam, her husband, was out of town all week again, and besides, I had gained a pound-and-a-half myself! I was also troubled to hear that Ruth had slept two or three afternoons, and I sensed that several of the others were troubled by that too. But all we did was say that it was sure better than sleeping five afternoons, like she used to. Jo hadn't been able to come at all because of another commitment, and I felt she was losing interest when I talked to her on the phone. And Helen was late. . .

Oh, I wish I could forget the whole thing and go to sleep! But, of course, I couldn't. Like a gerbil on its exercise wheel, I started around again. Maybe this whole 3D idea wasn't meant for us here in Rochester. Maybe. . .

Only the face of the clock could be seen in our darkened bedroom. I tried to keep my eyes from it, hoping I'd fall asleep, but periodically I'd peek at it and almost watch the night and my precious sleep time, ticking away.

I started thinking again. It was bad enough that I myself had gained weight, but knowing four others had too really bothered me. It was easier in Weight Watchers, when I hadn't known the women personally. I paid no attention to their weight gains. What did they matter to me? But tonight was different. It really bothered me that Mary Jane and Helen had both recorded gains. And Lois certainly did not seem as positive and vibrant as she had at the beginning. And then I began to wonder what *they* were thinking about *me* tonight, their minister's wife not able to diet.

Around and around the exercise wheel went. I was sorry that I had ever heard those three words linked together—diet, discipline and discipleship. I'd much rather fight this diet thing alone than fail in front of nine other women. I looked at the clock; it was after three.

The next thing I knew, the alarm was ringing. It couldn't be 6:30; I didn't feel like I had slept at all! And in truth, I had been dreaming about 3D. The exercise wheel had gone right on turning in my sleep; no wonder I felt so exhausted. I managed to get out of bed and wander downstairs to start breakfast and make school lunches. Bill came down thirty minutes later.

"Well, late one?" he said. "I'll bet you're good and tired this morning." And he went to the door, to get the morning paper. He was smiling, but it made me angry all over again, and I bit my lip to keep from replying the way I wanted to. Instead, I admitted that I had been awake half the night—

disturbed about the 3D meeting, trying to solve all the problems of the group by myself.

Bill let me wind down, and then said simply, "Sounds to me like you need some leadership in that group, if for no other reason than to end it after an hour or so." He sat down and turned to the sports page. "You can't just wander around in each other's problems for four hours and then go home and expect to get a good night's sleep," he remarked from behind the paper.

Ouch! He had hit right on target and in five seconds come up with what had eluded me half the night. But I could already sense what was coming next, and I wanted no part of it! "If you're suggesting that I lead that group, the answer is no. I need help in discipline desperately—*and* in diet! Besides, I've led enough things in that church! It's someone else's turn!" I got up quickly and started clearing the table. He hadn't said one word about my leading the group, but I knew what he was thinking. I yanked the dishwasher door open and jerked the top rack out.

"I wonder if the reason the East Dennis group went so well," Bill asked gently, "was because of the leadership Jane and Lenny brought to it?"

"I'm sure it did. They certainly knew something about what they were doing," I retorted. "And you know the disciplined lives they lead at the Community. That would make a great deal of difference in leading a group."

"Pray about it, Carol," Bill said simply. "Jane and Lenny would be the first to tell you that *God* made the group work at East Dennis, not their nutrition or diet expertise. You know, it could be God's will, and you need to stay open to that possibility." He turned to the editorial page. I said nothing. But I was so mad that it was a miracle I didn't break a plate, putting it in the dishwasher. And what made me even madder was that I sensed he was right—again.

We didn't talk any more about 3D after that morning session, and I did my best to forget the whole discussion in the days that followed. There was never a lack of things to do at home or at church, so I just wrapped myself up in the various needs around me. The week slipped by, and soon it was Tuesday again. Just the thought that we might end up talking until midnight made me want to skip the 3D meeting entirely. But I knew I had no choice.

It was a beautiful clear October evening, with a nip in the air foretelling the onset of winter. In the yard the trees were an array of color—copper and gold and deep red. The children had raced outside as soon as dinner was over, to get a little more play time in before bedtime. Peter had his yellow Tonka trucks moving the earth around; Betsy had an old pink blanket spread out with dolls and stuffed animals all over it, having a family picnic. Tim was riding his bike around the house.

Just as I was ready to walk across the yard to church, my dad and my brother, Brian, drove in. I was delighted. What a perfect excuse not to go to the 3D meeting! My father had retired the previous year and moved to Rochester to live close to us. Brian, thirteen, was my "little" brother. He often seemed more like a son to us and an older brother to the children. Unfortunately, my mother's premature death and my Dad's job transfer made it necessary for Brian to live with us until Dad could take an early retirement. As soon as Dad moved to Rochester and found a little apartment with Brian, just a mile-and-a-half down the road, they became part of our family and dropped in all the time.

"Hi, Sis!" Brian yelled out the open window, "where are you going?"

"Oh, I was just going to some meeting at church, but I'd love to visit with you and Dad instead," I said, turning and starting to walk towards their car.

"We're not coming to visit," Brian replied quickly. "We just wanted to know if the kids wanted to go for a swim before bed."

We had a family swim membership over at the Sheraton Motel, and the children were able to swim there twelve months a year in their enclosed pool.

"Oh, please, Mom, *please,* can we go?" Betsy pleaded, jumping up and down with excitement, totally forgetting about her doll's family picnic on the blanket.

"Me, too! I want to go swim with Brian," Peter yelled and ran over to the car, grabbing Brian's outstretched arm.

Dad didn't even bother to shut the engine off. We chatted while the kids raced in to get towels and swimsuits. In no time, they were out again, piling into the back seat, and off they went, waving. And with them went my excuse for skipping 3D.

I was late. Hurrying across the yard, I slipped into the church and up the stairs to the little chapel. We had decided the week before, to move into the chapel where we could have some privacy. Situated in the middle of the church, the library tended to be a high traffic zone. People who wanted to go into the church office had to go through the library; people who were counseling with Bill usually waited in the library; and anyone heading towards the choir loft or the sanctuary had to pass through there too.

I opened the chapel door, and found I was the last one to arrive. "Oh," Ruth remarked, "I thought you might be at the preschool meeting downstairs tonight."

"Preschool meeting? Oh my goodness, I forgot!" I said, clapping my hand over my mouth. I had just finished my term as chairman of the committee, and I was easing my way out, but I was expected to be there tonight. Preschool—there was the perfect excuse for not staying at 3D tonight. But now that I was here, I knew I couldn't run out on them.

"I'll go down in a little while after we share," I said. "The preschool meetings are always late in finishing anyway."

"Speaking of finishing late," Mary Jane remarked, "my John thinks *these* meetings go much too late. He finally drove the babysitter home at 11:15 last week and had to leave the children unattended. That didn't make him very happy, and he said he hoped that didn't happen again tonight!"

So Bill wasn't the only one. Helen and Ruth, too, were concerned about the same thing. And then Margaret spoke up. "You know, we might as well face it: what we really need for the group is a leader."

"I agree," Dee chimed in.

"And the other problem we have," Ruth stated, "is that no one wants to really speak up. I didn't get the help I needed last week, and I didn't help anyone else, I'm afraid. And what good is a group like that?" she asked bluntly.

Most of the others in the group were nodding and murmuring their assent. "Someone to lead would be a big help," Helen agreed. I glanced over at Dorcas, but she wasn't saying a word; in her own way, she was as resistant as I was. For she, too, could read the handwriting on the wall. A long, very uncomfortable silence fell over the group.

Norma broke it, as several eyes fell on her. "I wish I could lead this group," she said apologetically, "but there's no way I can. I signed an agreement with my other diet group, that I would not lead any other group for at least six months after I finished with them."

I had hoped Norma was the answer for us, but now that was out.

"How about you, Dorcas?" I asked. "You're a teacher and a good one; you could do a great job."

"You've got to be kidding! Me, the big flunky from every weight watching group in town, leading a diet group? It will be a major accomplishment for me just to stay in this group until the end of the program." She laughed. And then everyone else laughed with her, and that broke the tension. Someone suggested we pray about who should lead. A great idea, I thought; why hadn't it occurred to me?

But, before we could pray, Lois said, "Carol, as the senior minister's wife, aren't you the most likely one to lead the group?"

"Lois," I replied, so vehemently that I startled myself, as well as the others, "I'm *tired* of leading groups! Let someone else lead for a change."

The tenseness returned to the room, and I knew it was my fault. My attitude was lousy. Feeling a little sheepish about it, I said, "I guess we'd better ask God to help us to know His will about this."

All of us knew, of course, that God had to make the difference in this group. If He didn't, we might as well join all the other diet and self-help groups in the community. I felt chagrined that we had not gone to Him first.

There was quite a bit of silent prayer, then a few audible prayers. I'm not sure how long this prayer time went on, but something was happening to me during it. I was softening. I knew I had to give up my resistance and be willing to lead this group. Someone else prayed, "God, show us Your will, and then help us to do it."

After that prayer time, the way seemed very clear. The group asked me to lead, and I was pleased to say yes. And Dorcas said she was also willing to lead, if needed, which meant her heart had been changed too. We decided to try to lead the group as a team of two. This way, there would be an added check and balance, as two hearts were often better at hearing the Holy Spirit than one. Dual leadership was also being tried around us, both in public school education and in Sunday School. That sounded super to me. So , in spite of our discouragement and resistance as a group, God moved us on. The leaders were ready, the group was enthusiastic, and we were all aware of God's presence and direction in a new way.

We decided that our meetings should last only one hour.

We would all weigh in before meeting time and start right at eight. We also agreed to pray for each member of the group every day. Mary Jane volunteered to type up a prayer list for us with names and telephone numbers.

Just about then, I happened to notice the chapel door knob turn slowly, and the door open just a crack. Looking carefully, I thought I could see Bill, glancing in. "Come on in," I said, motioning with my hand. "We've had a great time tonight."

"Are you almost ready to go home?" he said with a big smile. "Or are you going to stay on until midnight again?"

"We are getting so organized, you won't believe us," Dorcas answered.

"You're right, I won't believe you," he laughed heartily.
He wasn't at all surprised to learn that Dorcas and I were 'elected' to be group leaders. "I sort of felt that that was the direction you should take," he admitted. That breakfast-table scene last week flashed through my mind at that moment. Bill winked at me.

He shared with the group his enthusiasm for their undertaking and felt it was an area of great need in the church. "There's a verse that says that discipline is painful for the moment but that later it will produce the fruit of righteousness." He looked up at our blank faces. "It's in Hebrews," he said, picking up the Bible on the altar. "Here, Hebrews 12:11."

I had read the book of Hebrews several times, but somehow I felt as though I was hearing that verse for the first time. And judging from the reactions of the others, they felt the same way.

Beverly made a suggestion: "Why don't we memorize a verse of Scripture every week?"

I swallowed hard. I had not been able to memorize Scripture since I was a young girl in Sunday School. And a quick glance around the room indicated I wasn't alone.

She suggested we start with the verse Bill had just quoted.

"It will be a big help to us, as we try to be more disciplined as a group."

Bill agreed wholeheartedly. "There are many things all through the Bible that talk about our need for leading disciplined lives, that God might be glorified in our bodies." He flipped through the pages, stopping here and there and reading a few verses.

"Would you be willing," I asked him, "to come in every week just for a few minutes, to share things like that with us?"

"Sure."

The end of a perfect evening. We felt like a real group now, adventuring together on a new path. And having Bill come in made us feel a part of the church instead of just a bunch of women meeting at church. God was having His way, after all.

7

Trusting

I felt excited and happy now as Tuesday evenings approached. I even looked forward to leading the group, and I sensed that much of the change in my attitude was directly attributable to the daily prayer—both mine for all the others in the group, and theirs for me. Our mutual commitment had turned out to be a lot harder than any of us expected; it was also producing unexpected results. None of us had had very much practice in laying aside our own cares and concerns, in order to fully concentrate on the needs of others, even for only a few minutes a day. But we were beginning to get the hang of it.

At first, I had resented the prospect of coming to know the other women's failures. I felt my own were enough for me to cope with; I did not want the responsibility of having to care about others, too. But I soon became deeply convicted of what an ugly attitude this was—about as far from Christ's as it was possible to get. And never mind spiritualizing it; I knew plenty of non-Christians who cared more about other people than I did.

I was sorry. I determined to care enough to take their needs to God, which was the very best care I could give.

God did not expect me to heal their weaknesses or carry their burdens. But He did expect me to take their needs to

Him. And what's more, they were doing the same thing with my needs. We were all part of a team, working together, to get our lives more under the control of God. It was not a chore but a privilege.

We were learning a great deal in a hurry—not points of doctrine but practical ways to put our faith in God to work in the most mundane things of daily life. It became more and more apparent to me that my Christianity still revolved almost entirely around me, rather than around Christ. Oh, of course, I brought the big things of my life to Him. But the little things— the shopping list, the order of the day's priorities—were still my domain. I did things my way and in my time, and God had very little to do with them. What did things like the way I made the beds each day, or cooked the meals, or sewed on buttons, have to do with God? He certainly had much bigger things in the world to be concerned about.

And yet I knew from the Bible that every hair on my head was numbered, and that not a sparrow fell to the ground without the Father in heaven being aware of it. I had always accepted those facts in my head, but I had no idea how to translate them into my life.

Now I was beginning to see that if He cared about the sparrow's fall, He would be interested in my shopping list. The small, personal concerns of my life and the greatness of God's love were finally coming together. The smallest, most insignificant details of my daily life were opportunities to glorify Him. Imagine eating, sewing, cooking and cleaning house to the glory of God!

Along with this new awareness, I was now becoming convicted of my disobedience in little things. The still, small voice which I had successfully ignored so many times, by telling myself that God couldn't possibly care about such small details, was becoming louder and clearer all the time. He *did* care— I was the one who didn't.

As I listened more closely now, I began to see how my family meals were cooked and planned according to how I happened to feel at the moment, instead of according to what He might want, or to His glory. For instance, if I happened to feel super, I would bake some pumpkin pie or chocolate chip cookies, or broil some steaks or make some home-made french fries. But if I didn't feel like bothering, then tuna casserole or sloppy joes would do just fine. God was showing me how unloving this was and how it not only gypped my family but also failed to glorify Him. I had to stop doing things so uncaringly and selfishly and start doing things to please God.

As this whole idea of doing even the littlest things to the glory of God—that is, *living* for Him—became clearer in my mind, I began to see why I had been so uncomfortable in my previous diet group. The emphasis of that group had been to help me become a better *me!* I dieted so I could wear nicer clothes, get more attention from my husband and family, and have a good self-image. It was me at the center, but the center of my life was supposed to be God.

The old way had worked. I felt a hundred percent better, I bought new clothes, my husband loved the new me, and people at church and everywhere else raved about how wonderful I looked. But where did God fit into all of this? He didn't! It was an ego trip—a self-glorifying experience which, if I was interested in drawing closer to God, was exactly what I did not need.

The main problem, of course, was not with the weight watching program; it was with me. I had always thrived on the attention of others, In fact, I felt, deep down, that I couldn't live without it. In high school I was a drum majorette; now I was a minister's wife. All kinds of ups and downs in my life could be explained by the amount of attention and acceptance I was enjoying. But it was a trap.

I was finally beginning to understand that my acceptance had to be found in God—not in how I looked or what I weighed. And if I was convicted that my willful self-indulgence in the food department, and my refusal to say no to self, was not pleasing to God, then I should change for that reason, not for vanity's sake, or the sake of a better self-image.

But just because the picture was clearer to me now, it didn't make it any easier. It was just as hard to resist a piece of banana cream pie. And it still wasn't easy to discipline myself to pray every day for the group members. It would generally take only ten minutes or so to go down the prayer list, but I was finding that I couldn't stay with God for even that long, to intercede for the needs of others. Like a willful little child, my mind would persist in wandering off to what I had to do that day. God had obviously brought 3D into my life for more reasons than dieting.

How thankful I was for that time, a year before, when Cay and Judy had suggested that I consider assuming a three-month discipline of not criticizing Bill. That was what it had taken to break my obnoxious and ultimately destructive habit of pick, pick, pick, that was pervading our marriage and home. For me, that had been the forerunner of the whole 3D concept. I reminded myself that three months had been a very small price to pay for what had happened. So when it was tough to stick to these new disciplines, I would remind myself of how free I now felt because of the disciplines the previous May. And I'd go on—expecting the same sort of change to take place in me. Others in the group were also struggling, but as we shared together on Tuesday nights, I found that they, too, were learning about the blessings of being disciplined. And, not only were we learning together, but we were enjoying just being together. Our hour together on Tuesday nights didn't seem nearly long enough any more. On Sunday mornings after the church service, we would gather around in the narthex and catch up on each other's diets or sewing or house projects.

Nor was it unusual to answer the phone and hear, "Hi, this is Helen. I couldn't wait until Tuesday to tell you what happened to me today!" In these few months together, a bond of love in Christ was being established among us. It was easy now to call and ask one of the others for special prayer; we were not ashamed to be needy and share our most seemingly foolish problems. For example, whom else could one call to ask for prayer that one not eat the Swiss chocolate almond ice cream in the freezer, while everyone was out of the house?

There had been very few people in our church with whom I had ever shared much of myself. I had an image of what a good minister's wife should be, and a part of that image was to be able to handle small problems myself—like dieting and cleaning house. I was sure they would not be interested in all my petty grievances or even understand that those things would bother me, But I was wrong. Just the opposite was true. As I shared my personal needs, the women felt much closer to me.

One of them confessed one night in the group that she had been scared to death of sharing her small needs in front of "the minister's wife" for fear she would be rejected. But she lost her fear, when she heard I had some of the same feelings. We laughed together and saw how silly all of this was, and what ridiculous images we had of one another. After that, I wondered if this wasn't indeed one of the Devil's ways of keeping Christians from getting too close to one another, by letting them believe they would be unacceptable to one another, if the truth about themselves were known.

New relationships were springing up within our group every week. Mary Jane told one night of how she had judged me two years before, because of an episode with the Christian education committee. They had asked me to teach the senior high Sunday School class and had assigned me a topic, giving me specific materials to use. I had not been comfortable with the materials and had requested permission to use something else. "I was furious that you would dare question the material we had picked out," Mary Jane recalled. "After all, I was a school teacher, and you weren't. What right did you have to override our decision?" She paused, and shook her head at the memory. "From that night on, I decided I really didn't like you, even if you were the new minister's wife."

"Wow," I said, awed by this confession, "and I never even realized anything was wrong. You've always been pleasant to me."

"Oh, yes, pleasant, but not really friendly," she said, laughing. "But now, since I've been in this group with you and praying for you every day, I feel totally different. Please forgive me for holding such a silly grudge against you all this time."

I went over and threw my arms around her and gave her a big hug. She threw her arms around me, and there we stood, both laughing and wiping tears from our eyes at the same time.

After that we were more open and honest than ever. We talked about our buried grudges and resentments. Many of us had kidded ourselves that they didn't matter anyway, but deep down we knew that these things did seriously affect our relationships with others. So, by the gentle leading of the Holy Spirit, we were finding healing and renewal.

Dee deeply resented Sam's job, which required him to be out of town so much. And there seemed to be a clear connection between that anger and the hard time she had with her weight. "When I'm lonely, I eat—and especially at night after the children go to bed." she admitted. And several of the women in the group encouraged her to call them when she felt like that—before she ate the chocolate cake or dish of ice cream. And each of us could pray a lot more specifically for Dee after that.

Beverly, who tended to be very quiet and rather standoffish, told about how hurt she had been as a young girl when her mother died. "I guess, way back there, I decided that I'd better just pull back from people and make it on my own and not get too close to anyone again!" she said.

Just that little bit of sharing from Bev made us all feel closer to her. We were all beginning to see that these small, seemingly insignificant things were prevalent in all of us and did indeed affect our relationships with one another. It was as though we were all imprisoned in invisible, solitary confinement cells, afraid to reveal ourselves beyond the most superficial level. And yet, when we did, the love of God and the caring that poured out among us were incredible !

The 3D meetings got better every week. Now everyone was being open, and the flow of the Spirit in the group seemed really good. And then, one night in early December, Bill dropped what, to me, felt like a one-ton bomb. He asked us if we thought we were reaching out enough to others. "Yes, like never before!" one of the group exclaimed, and several others quickly agreed. Bill listened, as we then took turns expounding on the ways we had reached out to one another.

Suddenly he cut across the testimony. "I'm delighted with what's happening in the group, but what about outside of the group?"

Gulp. I wasn't thinking about beyond the group. I was just so glad to see what was happening in the group. For crying out loud! What does he expect in just three months?

"Have you invited other women in the church who have some of the same problems you do, to join your group?" he asked pointedly.

That made me mad! But I bit my lip, and decided to wait until I got home to let him know how I felt. I wasn't about to expose my anger in front of the group—I couldn't be *that* honest!

There was an uncomfortable silence for several moments. Then Helen quietly spoke up, a sense of conviction in her voice. "I'm sure you are picking up something that we need to face up to," she took a deep breath and went on. "I can see that it would be very easy to get comfortable in this group and even become a clique—but we can't afford to. We are only a very small part of Parkminster's women, and there are lots more than ourselves we need to be concerned about."

Dee spoke next. "I've often felt funny about being a part of this group, when I don't even belong to your church. And I've had the thought that there might be women in this church who deserved to be a part of this group, instead of me."

"Don't feel that way, Dee!" I blurted out. "We're glad to have you as a part of this group, and it doesn't matter a bit that you go to another church." Brother, was I going to say a few things to Bill when I got home!

But for some reason the rest of the group didn't seem nearly as upset as I was; in fact, I was shocked at their positive response to what he was saying.

"As much as I hate the thought of having the group change or enlarge," Lois said, "I think we really do have to think about others in the church who might want to be a part of this group. And without thinking very hard, I can come up with three or four friends, who I know would join tomorrow if they could."

"It scares me, too," Ruth confessed, "and I'm afraid we might lose the closeness and trust we've found these months. But I guess we'll have to trust God again, won't we?"

Bill nodded approvingly. "I understand your apprehension, but I believe it is time to invite others. God has been changing your lives—more than you ever expected, and in a remarkably short time, when you stop to think about it. And it happened because you've trusted Him and been obedient to what He's required of you. But now you need to share that. He won't stop working just because the group gets bigger. Remember, He is a very big God! "

The others laughed at that, but I was still smoldering inside at the mere thought of a change in the group. And Dorcas, I noticed, was conspicuously silent also; I was sure she felt as I did.

Finally I had to speak. "Well, you've certainly given us something to think about, and we will. But with the holidays practically on top of us, we probably won't have time to really consider it until after the New Year."

But Bill would not be put off. "I think after the New Year is when you should begin with new members, not just consider it."

At this point I gladly could have shouted at him, yet somehow I kept silent and even kept smiling. But just wait till we got home. . .

Dorcas broke the tense silence. "Well, speaking for myself, it seems to me that we have considered it tonight, and, frankly, I feel that we are supposed to do something about it—now. I know I've been convicted by what Bill has said to us."

Dorcas! I looked at her, feeling almost betrayed. But with my own emotions so obviously distraught, I decided I'd better leave the rest of the plans and discussion to the others. I sat through it all, but was withdrawn, trying to figure out why I was reacting so to this suggestion. I had begun to calm down inside, and now I was shocked at the violence of my initial reaction.

I was relieved when the meeting broke up; I needed to get in touch with what was happening deep within me, and I sensed it was something I wasn't to bring up in the whole group. So instead of going home, I decided to wait in the church library to see if I might see Bill between his counseling appointments. I needed some counseling pretty badly myself.

Confused, I began to seek the Lord's help. And for no apparent reason, all of a sudden I found myself thinking about our former church in Bridgeport. And then a specific scene came to mind: it was our last morning in Bridgeport. Our furniture had already left for Rochester, and we were spending the night at Betty Rutan's home. I woke up almost before it was dawn outside and was suddenly overcome with inexplicable grieving. It made no sense at all. I knew we were in God's will to move; we'd said our goodbyes and were looking forward to our new church. But suddenly I was so overcome with the thought of leaving, that I just sat on my side of the bed and sobbed. I had my hand over my mouth, but I woke Bill anyway. "What's the matter, hon, can't you sleep anymore?"

"Sleep? Who can sleep when we are about to leave the people we love so much!" I cried. "And it doesn't seem to bother you at all—don't you have any feelings?"

Apparently sensing that nothing he could say would help, he came over and sat next to me, put his arm around me and let me cry it out on his shoulder.

What a curious thing to think of, after all these years! And then I saw the connection: I was having the same kinds of feelings tonight, just thinking about changing the makeup of our 3D group. In an instant, I saw how much I put my security in relationships—first at Bridgeport and now in the 3D group— and how comparatively little in Christ. Tied in with my fear of rejection, this situation felt explosive to me. Acceptance meant everything to me, and now here was a group that accepted me—overweight and undisciplined—a group that I could really be *me* in, and now it was being taken from me.

It wasn't all clear to me, and I was anxious for Bill's help in putting the pieces in place, but as I waited for his door to open I became aware of another grief—only this one was not my own. For the first time in my life, I thought of how Jesus must feel, and must have felt all these years, as I consistently turned to others for my security, instead of to Him. Now I *really* had something to feel sorry about!

By the time Bill finished his appointment, my anger had dissipated, and I was a little sheepish at what had happened earlier. When I shared it all with Bill, he was surprised at first to hear that the whole Bridgeport thing had surfaced again but quickly saw the same connection. "God has been trying for a long time to get you to put your trust in Him. But He's also been patiently waiting for you to reach a place where you would be ready. You're ready now."

8

A New Beginning

The Christmas season, 1973, came on us quickly, and the activities were in full swing both around the house and the church. All of our holiday schedules were such that we had decided not to meet for 3D again, until the first Tuesday of the new year. As much as I missed the fellowship of the group, I was grateful to have one less meeting to go to. There was so much to do. In addition to our family's preparation, there were the church's needs—decoration, planning carol sings, baking cookies and breads, making food baskets for shut-ins, and producing special pageants by the various youth groups. And then no sooner would Christmas be over, than plans and preparations would begin for the big New Year's Eve dinner and service at church.

In our household the traditional sign that the season was upon us was when Bill and the children went on their annual Christmas tree expedition. And back they would come, with the biggest and fullest tree they could find tied to the top of our station wagon. This year, as usual, Bill had been too extravagant, and at least a foot would have to be chopped off the top; in fact, the branches had to be trimmed before it would fit through the front door! But I had to admit that I, too, loved a full Christmas tree, and so I put out of mind the thought of all those pine needles in the living room carpet for months after Christmas, and joined in.

While Bill and the children lugged the big boxes of decorations down from the attic, I began selecting the Christmas Hummels from the bookcase shelves—shelves high up, out of the reach of little hands, for these delicate figures had become very special to me over the years. The soft, hand-painted features made them just perfect for Christmas scenes. I loved especially the figures of Mary and the Baby Jesus. She was kneeling with her arms spread, as if to say, "See, my son, the Holy One of God," and her eyes were closed in thanks to her heavenly Father. The Baby Jesus lay on the hay with a white cloth under him; his eyes were open and bright, his hands responding to his mother's presence. Beside his bed, I placed the little figure of a sheep, which watched Him intently, its eyes fixed on the bed and its ears sticking out, listening. In my collection I had only two kings, and these I placed just off to one side at a respectful distance. One, a black man with a turban and footwear that laced halfway up his legs, stood with one hand on his sword, and the other holding out a gift of frankincense. The second king was an older man, with a beard and a crown-shaped hat. He was kneeling, offering a little chest of gold to the mother and child. Surrounding the manger scene, I put little angels playing musical instruments. And once the last angel was in place, I straightened up and surveyed the scene. Now let the celebration begin!

To a weak-willed glutton, Christmas is an endless procession of goodies—fancy cookies, spiced punch bowls, rich creamy eggnog, and cranberry breads! It was customarily impossible for me to diet over the holidays; gaining weight seemed as much a part of the holiday season as getting a Christmas tree. But somehow I had the feeling of its being different this year; the battle seemed easier. And I knew that the extra will power I now seemed to have was coming out of the group; for even though we were not meeting together, there were still nine friends praying for me every day.

In fact, everything was going beautifully over the holidays—until the Sunday after Christmas. I was sitting in church, waiting for the service to begin and looking over the bulletin, when one announcement jumped out at me.

> Any women who might be interested in joining the group that has been dealing with problems of diet, discipline and discipleship should meet in the chapel on Tuesday, January 7, at 8 P.M.

With a jolt I realized that I had completely put out of mind the reality that our group was going to be enlarged the next time we met. Never again would it just be the ten of us. And sure enough, just thinking about it brought up again those same feelings of fear and betrayal and—but the difference was that now I recognized them and could turn them right over to the Lord before I went down under them. So I prayed, "Jesus, help me now," and set my will to trust Him, and to be obedient to His leading. Once I had done that, I felt peace return, and it remained through the rest of the service.

January 7th, 7:45 P.M.: A dozen chairs in the little chapel had been removed from the neat rows facing the altar and arranged into a small circle. The old "3Ders" had arrived early for a quick weight check-in. The news was bad but not awful for most of us—two or three pounds up—and not nearly as bad as it had been in previous years, for which we were all rejoicing. There was a warm feeling amongst us.

"Looks like three weeks off is just a little more than most

of us disciplined dieters can handle," Dee called toward the scale which was located in the east hall.

"That's for sure," I called back, marking my two-pound gain on the old chart.

"Boy, have I missed the group," Helen said, "and more than just to check my weight!"

"Me, too," remarked Dee. "And I didn't see any of you during the holidays." She had worked hard at St. Helen's Catholic Church over the holidays.

As we waited for the newcomers, we took turns telling what had been happening without diets and disciplines since last we met. Though most of us had seen each other fairly frequently at the holiday events, it never seemed appropriate to bring up 3D. Yet now we laughed and talked together as if we had never been apart. We had left the chapel door ajar, half-watching for newcomers, but having really forgotten that they were coming. All of a sudden the door opened, and a voice interrupted us. "Is this where the diet and discipline group is meeting?"

I looked towards the door. It was Judy Litt! What in the world was she doing here? She was stunning—tall, slender and stylish.

"Yes, Judy," I managed, "come on in," and I tried to smile encouragingly to conceal my dismay.

Three more women followed closely behind. All four of them looked as though they could have stepped out of fashion magazines. The warmth that had been flowing through the chapel moments before was gone, and in its place, a chill of lack of trust settled over the room.

Mary Jane offered to get more chairs to enlarge the circle, and as more newcomers arrived, we needed five, then ten, and then twenty. Women were filing in at an unbelievable pace, one right after another, and before long the circle was touching the altar rail at one end of the room and the folding doors at the other. When some really fat women finally joined the circle, I felt a little guilty to be so delighted to see them. But for a few minutes there, it had looked as if the thin ones were going to take over 3D.

I was astounded at the turn-out; by eight o'clock there were thirty-nine women in the room! We squeezed together closely, many keeping their winter coats on and pocket books in their laps, making the circle seem even tighter. There was a strained, uncomfortable atmosphere in the room; I could sense the feelings that were floating around—fear, anxiety, jealousy, and more than a little judgment.

A hush fell over the group a few minutes after eight, and all eyes turned towards me. I was speechless, even prayerless, but I finally managed a "Jesus, help me!" under my breath. Then I had no choice but to trust Him and begin to talk.

First, I shared about my experience in the nationally known diet group. That seemed to crack the ice a little, and looking around I recognized several women whom I had seen attending those meetings. But there was still a strong "Okay, show me" attitude in the room. My hands were clasped in my lap, and I was twisting my engagement ring around and around on my finger. My hand was stone cold, so my ring moved freely and probably could have fallen off without too much effort.

"Unfortunately," I went on, "soon after I had reached my weight goal and graduated, the pounds slowly began to creep back on. Nor was this the first time—in fact, it was a depressing pattern of mine—that long months of painful dieting were wiped away in just a few weeks. And as before, I had promised myself that this time it would be different. After all, I had become quite learned on calories and carbohydrates, and just which foods did what. But all the head knowledge I possessed was powerless, when it came up against my strong determination to indulge myself." The group knew exactly what I was talking about, and several heads were nodding around the circle.

"Something was missing from my experience in the diet group. It had been a tremendous help to me—I did lose thirty-seven pounds! But, when I went back to rejoin last May, something inside of me balked. I just couldn't do it." I had the feeling that others in this group had experienced the same thing, and that perhaps that was why they were here tonight.

"And then God spoke to me through a red smile-face painted on a Sunday school partition. The words under the face said, 'Smile, God has the answer.' And He did, though it was nearly a year before He showed it to me."

I went on briefly to tell about the start of 3D and also about the positive impression I had of the disciplined life in the Community of Jesus. "I knew I was undisciplined and not just in the area of food. What I saw on Cape Cod seemed to me to somehow contain the answer."

Abruptly the words ran out. I stopped, not knowing what else to say. Dorcas smoothly picked up the discussion and went on. As she got into what she was saying, I was again aware of what a blessing it was to have two leaders, instead of one. Way back when God had practically forced the two of us to become co-leaders, I had had no idea how it was going to turn out, but how many times I had been grateful since—like tonight. For one thing, no meeting depended all on one person. When the flow of words dried up for one of us, it seemed as if the other leader. was just ready to start. God had known what He was doing that night, and here I had thought it was only because we were both so resistant!

"I have joined and quit more diet groups and spent more money trying to lose weight in the past year than probably anyone else in this room!" Dorcas exclaimed, to a ripple of knowing laughter. Apparently she was not the only one in the join-quit category. "I kept thinking I could do it myself, once I had gotten a little start from a group, but it never worked for more than a few weeks. Yet, during these past ten or twelve weeks, something has been happening in me. I've begun to understand that it is part of God's plan that we help one another, instead of being so determined to do it ourselves. And that has put dieting in a whole new ballpark for me."

As the two of us continued, back and forth, illustrating from our own experiences, what tension remained in the room perceptibly relaxed. "I have come to admit and recognize that I am an undisciplined person," I concluded. "The 3D group has been a real help to my life in Christ. I am learning for the first time how to really *care* for someone else besides myself." There, I had said it! Openly and honestly. And it felt good.

We opened the meeting for a time of sharing then, and what a blessing that turned out to be! There was no pretense, no phoniness, just honesty. Ruth told of her unfinished draperies and bedspread, and lots of the women could identify with her. "They had been sitting around our bedroom for two years waiting to be finished, and during the weeks I was in 3D, I finished them! So you can imagine how delighted my husband was to see them on the windows and on the bed instead of in a corner of the bedroom. The prayers and support of the 3D group did it—I just know they did."

Mary Jane spoke next. "I haven't done that great in the weight department, but lots else has happened to me. I didn't know any of the women in this group very well, and those I did know, I didn't particularly like." Several laughed at her candor. "But when you pray for someone every day, your petty gripes disappear. Before I knew it, not only did I like them all, but God gave me a real love for them—His love." Tears filled her eyes, and her voice broke. "I just can't tell you how different I feel," she concluded, smiling.

I felt tears welling up in my own eyes and saw them in a number of others' eyes as well. Helen got up and went to get a box of Kleenex, leaving the chapel door open to relieve the stuffiness of the small room. That helped to relax the group even more, although almost all the tension had already lifted. She came back and handed the Kleenex box to Mary Jane, who passed it on.

Then Ann Groves spoke up. "When can I become a part of this group?"

"Well—" I started, not knowing quite how to answer.

"This is an answer to prayer to me," Ann added. "I *need* a group like this."

I knew Ann, from working with her on the preschool committee. She took a very active role in the church, although her husband was not involved at all. "I'm ready to start in a group like this tomorrow," she said and sat down.

And indeed there was a definite feeling in the room of "Let's get on with it." Dorcas and I looked at one another, a little amazed. "How many of you feel like Ann, that a group like this is something you are really interested in?" I asked. Every single hand went up! "But you haven't even heard what we do in the group, or what disciplines are required."

"Maybe after they hear the requirements, they won't be quite as interested!" Dorcas said with a smile.

"First," I said, drawing myself up to my most imposing posture, "you have to be on time for every meeting. In fact, you have to come fifteen minutes before the scheduled time, in order to get weighed in. And everyone must weigh in, weight problem or not. Also, you must commit yourself to come every week, unless, of course, there is a genuine emergency for you." Still no resistance in the room.

Dorcas took it from there. "We have also made a commitment to one another to pray at a specific time each day without fail for everyone else in the group." With this, she held up a copy of our prayer list, so everyone could see it. "Praying for one another has changed every one of our attitudes as dramatically as Mary Jane's."

Marilyn Christopher, a petite woman weighing not more

than a hundred pounds, brought up a concern. "I've come tonight because I need help in my spiritual life. But I'm sitting here wondering how I am ever going to find time to pray for thirty-nine women every day, when I can't find time to pray for my four children!"

I smiled, because that same thought had crossed my mind just a few moments before. "I don't really know, Marilyn. We never dreamed we'd have this many here tonight. God will have to show us how it is going to work."

I took a fresh look around the circle. There were Sue Clark, a very attractive young mother and a newcomer to the church; Jan Brule, a rather stocky, pretty woman who was a head nurse at Strong Memorial Hospital; Barbara Cole, the new church secretary; and other familiar faces. I knew their names, but I felt as though I hardly knew them beyond that. Suddenly, I felt as if I was on the brink of knowing them better and letting them know me better, and that felt good to me.

But how was it all going to work? Bill and I talked about it after the meeting that night, and neither of us felt right about just having one, great big group. The openness and trust had just begun in the small group of ten, and it definitely seemed that this was what God wanted for us. We both agreed that it was indeed God's direction, and He had blessed it, so we'd better stay with it and have two or three small groups, instead of one big one.

"But who is going to lead if we have three groups?" I asked.

"Guess," Bill said with a half smile.

"Oh. . . How in the world will we ever find the time?" I groaned.

"Well, remember, 3D is God's idea," he laughed, "so He'll just have to make more time for you and Dorcas."

9

"I Want to be Myself!"

From January, 1974, until the end of March, there were three diet, discipline and discipleship groups meeting in the church every week. Beverly Evans helped Dorcas and me with the leadership responsibilities, filling in and replacing either of us when necessary, which was often enough so that we really counted on her.

One of the first things we invested in was a big hospital-type scale for weighing in. Although the cost was well over a hundred dollars, there was no problem raising the money from the members of the groups. In fact, it was even suggested that we take a weekly offering, to purchase the things we might need, though there was little that was necessary for a diet group beyond an accurate scale! Now there could be no more shaving a pound or two by shifting towards the right front or leaning towards the back left corner. Every quarter of a pound would register, no matter what you did ! Naturally, everyone was excited at first with a new, highly accurate scale, but in the weeks to come there were more than a few of us who occasionally wished for our old bathroom standby back!

At one of the evening groups, I was busy marking the weight chart, as everyone came in, when I noticed that Barbara Cole had slipped in and not said a word about her weight.

"How'd you do this week, Barb?" I said, glancing over at her and preparing to mark it on the chart.

"I didn't weigh in," she finally replied.

"Oh, well, the scale's empty now; you can go ahead." But Barbara made no move to go to the hall. Puzzled, I stopped what I was doing and looked at her. She looked like she was angry, but that couldn't—

"Why do I have to weigh in, anyway?" She *was* angry.

"Because," I answered calmly, too surprised at first to get angry myself, "it's a discipline every one of us in 3D agreed to." And for a split second, I wondered why *did* she have to weigh in? Why do any of these women with such nice figures have to bother weighing in? But something inside me checked that response, before I could speak it.

Barbara still made no move to get up. I sensed that she might have picked up my slight hesitation, so I repeated my direction to her with some firmness in my voice. "Go on out now, Barb, and weigh in."

"I don't think I should have to weigh in, if I don't want to."

"Well, none of us particularly enjoys weighing in either, but that's the direction God has given us. So, be obedient."

She contemplated a further reply, then got up and stalked out to the scale in the hall. But the next thing I heard was her berating Dorcas, who was doing the weighing-in, about how stupid it was to have everyone weigh in! I shook my head, got up, and went out to the scale, speaking even before Dorcas could respond.

"Barbara, your attitude is wrong!" I said, surprised at how strong the words came out. "I just spoke to you in the chapel about why everyone weighs in—because it's God's direction—and it is totally unnecessary for you to go on like this now with Dorcas."

Inside, I was wincing. Barbara worked in the church office,

and I certainly didn't want to affect my relationship with her. But as much as I hated this confrontation, it was necessary to insist that she weigh in like everyone else. She weighed a perfect 110 pounds, according to her card, and I could not imagine for the life of me what she was reacting to.

She took her shoes off slowly, indicating she was going to get on the scale, so I returned to the chapel. Minutes passed, and another member came in from the hall, reported her weight loss, and sat down. Wait a minute, where was Barb? Had she left the building? Had I been too strong on her? I felt awful. Should I have excused her from weighing in? But had I done that. . . a movement caught the corner of my eye. It was Barbara coming back, not to the seat she had occupied before, but to one closer to the outside door.

"What was your weight loss, Barb?" I asked, trying to make it sound casual.

"I gained—a pound and a half" she shot back, not raising her head to even look at me.

I marked her gain on the large, poster-type chart which had a place beside each name to mark the weight change for each week. And at the bottom was a place to total the group's combined weight loss for the week. Though everyone else in the group had a minus figure beside her name, none of us gave another thought to her gain—after all, even at 111½ she looked far better than most of the rest of us.

We prayed and started the meeting but had hardly begun, when I noticed that Barbara was crying. Lord, what do I do now? Then she spoke. "I—I'm really sorry for my weight gain. . . it affects the group's total," and then she began to sob.

"Don't be silly, Barb! I wish I could gain one and a half pounds and look like you do!" one of the heavy group members said, trying to get her to smile.

But she cried unconsolably, her upset far surpassing the situation itself. Again she tried to talk. "I'm sorry. . . ,"

"Why are you so upset?" I asked. "It can't be over a measly pound and a half."

"Everyone here lost weight tonight but me—that's awful!" And again she sobbed, burying her face in her hands.

Why had I ever made her weigh in? If only I had known—known what? Now my own emotions were getting involved, and I was losing my sense of any direction from God. I didn't want to see her so upset. Lord, help her! Lord, help me! The room was silent, and it felt as if everyone else was praying, too.

"I never should have joined 3D!" Barbara burst out. "Dick and I had really begun to find something in this church that we had never known before. And, from what I had heard about it, I thought 3D would help me, But instead, I'm ruining the group!"

"Now that is *not* true," Dorcas replied emphatically, "not true at all!" But there was a wall now between Barbara and the rest of the group, as if she had sealed herself off from us, brick by brick. She would not accept the assurance of the group, no matter what any of them said.

Then one of the women hit upon the thing that finally broke through the wall. "Are you afraid that the group will reject you because you are the only one that didn't lose weight?"

Startled, Barbara looked at the woman and nodded. Her thoughts were finally exposed, and it was okay. "I always worked hard at doing whatever the group I was in was doing. That way I knew I would be accepted. And if I couldn't, I'd drop out rather than fail." She went on and expressed her panic with this group. "Dieting has never been much of a problem with me. I've always been able to maintain my weight very close to what I've wanted it to be. But I've never been weighed in by anyone every single week like this. And to tell the truth, I've been a wreck every day just thinking about it. I find myself hopping on the scale twice a day at home, watching every quarter of a pound! Dick gets so upset with me. But I've seen how much every little quarter of a pound means to most of you, and how hard it is for you to lose each week. I didn't want to hurt the group!"

Now I was beginning to understand what all was going on inside of her. Because she was thin to begin with, she had felt perfectly acceptable in the group. It was as if she had passed some qualification for membership in her own mind. But any weight gain meant to her that she was failing both herself and the group. And she was irrationally scared to death the group would reject her. At this point, one of the heaviest women in the group spoke up and said a very beautiful thing to her.

"I think there's something I ought to tell you. I've never felt accepted anywhere, because I'm so fat, and that includes church groups. I'm always sure I'll be rejected. I walk into a group, and I'm afraid no one will want to sit near me or talk to me, because I'm so fat!" She paused. "But now I see that you are just as afraid of rejection as I am, and the truth is that it doesn't have much to do with whether we are fat or thin. We are all scared of other peoples' opinions of us."

She went over and put her arm around Barbara, who cried freely, and then started laughing. "You know, I just can't believe this! I really can't believe it! I feel like someone just unlocked the door and let me go free."

Good grief! I was crying again, it was so beautiful; but then, so were most of the others. There was a fresh burst of laughter, as someone started the Kleenex box around the circle. And then others in the group confessed their fears of being rejected by the group, either because of their weight problems or their disorganized homes, or because they weren't so spiritually on top of things as they thought others might expect them to be. I was free to share my own fears of rejection and what a hold they had on me as I went into new situations.

It was clear that there wasn't a choice between any of us,

fat or thin, leader or member. And all this had come to pass because one attractive, thin woman had gained a pound and a half. And to think that in the beginning I had regretted it coming up! God knew what He was doing, and it didn't matter if I didn't. After all, He was in charge, wasn't He? I needed to be willing to let people be uncomfortable, and be uncomfortable myself, to allow the Spirit of God to touch wherever He willed, using whatever method He chose. He took very good care of Barbara, and she was none the worse for all that crying; in fact, the whole thing had helped her *and* the group immeasurably, in spite of my ineptitude.

Similar situations occurred week after week in these three groups. And in each instance, we were in uncharted waters, praying much and leaning heavily on the Holy Spirit, for His wisdom and discernment. Much practical teaching was coming out of such seemingly petty experiences as thin people weighing in. But it certainly wasn't insignificant to realize, for instance, that you lived in constant fear of being rejected, or that you basically didn't trust other people, which several women discovered about themselves. That big hospital scale, which some of us called the "gray monster", was bringing up all sorts of opportunities for spiritual growth.

Another significant thing happened in the group that met upstairs on Tuesday evenings. The room itself was rather dismal—dirty gray walls, one funny-shaped window with a fan half blocking it, the worst of the church's folding chairs (most of them half broken, it seemed) and an ugly old beige rug on the floor. The fluorescent light fixture was broken, and the bare tubes were too bright and harsh for the smallness of the room. I remember Diane Frazier commenting that it felt as though we were in a police lineup room waiting to be interrogated, instead of a church diet group. But we did our best to forget the ugliness of the room and have good meetings in spite of it.

On this particular Tuesday night, Helen McClurg was talking. One of the original ten, Helen was a part of this new group, along with Ruth Bailey. As usual, Helen's whispery voice was hard to hear, especially if she was sharing something rather personal or difficult, which was the case this night. I can't remember what she was sharing, but she seemed to be talking into her lap in this barely audible voice, pausing after every three or four words. Before I knew what I was doing, strong words were coming out of my mouth.

"Helen, *when are you going to grow up?*" The words shocked her, and me too. It was as if I'd had the thought outloud. I immediately tried to soften it. "I really think you need to stop talking and acting like a little girl and grow up into the woman of God you are supposed to be." The words were still strong, although not quite as loud.

Dorcas spoke up then, for which I was deeply grateful. The room had tensed up some, and it seemed as though a few in the group were embarrassed for Helen and perhaps upset with me.

"I think Carol is absolutely right," Dorcas said. "I have been in groups with you for many months, and I have often felt that your soft, tender voice is very little-girlish. You are raising three teenage boys at home, aren't you? Is that the voice you use with them?"

"Oh, no!" she quickly answered, with some volume in her voice. "I yell at John and the boys a lot at home." The group laughed at the quickness of her reply.

"Then maybe you need to ask God why it is that here at church, you come across so meek and mild, with a voice so timid it can't be heard," Dorcas went on.

Helen nodded her head but I wasn't sure she had understood at all what we were saying. She never spoke again for the rest of the meeting time.

I could hardly keep my mind on the rest of the group,

worrying about whether I had done the right thing by confronting Helen so strongly right in the group. There was no question that there was an uncomfortable apprehension in the group after that. It had not been our style in the 3D groups to speak so strongly and directly to someone. I remained upset inside through the remainder of the meeting, and when the last woman walked out after the group, I closed the door, sinking fast.

"What on earth ever made me speak so strongly to Helen?" I moaned to Dorcas. "I'll bet I've lost some friends tonight."

"I think you were obeying the Holy Spirit. Helen *needed* it. What you were showing her was real love—tough love. I don't think she would have heard it at all, if it had been said lovingly and softly."

And Dorcas went on to recall several small-group experiences where a whole group had spoken to Helen about talking up more. "Everyone had pointed it out—lovingly—but nothing has changed."

No matter what Dorcas said that night, I still felt totally wrong about what had happened. I was in self-pity up to my ears. Now I was the one who was refusing to listen to the truth.

Bill immediately sensed my "down", when I got home. I told him what had happened, and he spoke to me even more strongly than Dorcas. "God has placed you in a position of leadership in that group, not because you wanted to be a leader, but because God put you there. And if His Holy Spirit is going to help you lead His way, you have to be willing to say what your heart tells you is necessary, regardless of how it comes across." He paused. "And if you refuse to speak because you are afraid someone might not want to hear it or like it, you are wrong!"

And I saw that I didn't care as much about Helen and how she was taking what I had said, as I was caring about me.

"I think you said exactly what God gave you to say," he went on, "and what's more, I think it needed to be said strongly. Your trouble is, you're really more concerned about people liking you than helping someone like Helen grow in Christ."

I clammed up. I was not about to discuss my old fear of rejection again. I just wanted to forget that whole episode. It was pointless to talk about it further. He would see! Next Tuesday night, the only people who would show up for the group would be Dorcas and me.

The first thing the next morning, Dorcas called me and said Helen had called, crying, and wanted to talk to both of us. I knew it! What a mess I'd made!

But as it turned out, it was not a mess at all. Helen shared lots and lots of things that she needed to share. God had really used that confrontation to open up areas of her life which needed healing. I was awed at what God did in her life that day and throughout the rest of the week. We met with her, then Bill met with her, and most important, God met with her, in a new and exciting way, and she practically "grew up" right before our eyes.

The next Tuesday night Helen was in the best shape ever. She could hardly wait to tell how God had spoken to her and healed her of many fears and hurts. Like so many of the rest of us, she feared rejection. "I guess I've had an image of a good Christian—it was someone who never spoke loudly or raised her voice."

No wonder she had looked so blankly at me that night. I had jumped out of the "good Christian" box by speaking so strongly and loudly.

"And at home," Helen smiled, "where I have to raise my voice so frequently, I felt like a total failure as a Christian. So I tried to be someone else at church, and everyone likes little girls, so that seemed like a safe place to hide."

"What I really want," she said, drawing herself up straight

in her chair and looking at each woman in the circle, "is to be myself." Her voice was strong and clear now. "And with God's help, I'm going to be." We practically cheered. She was so much freer than we had ever seen her. "And I want you all to tell me," she concluded, "whenever I sink back into that little-girl syndrome." We all laughed and promised to tell her.

Jan Brule spoke up after that. "I can't tell you what a help it was to me last week, to learn that Helen raised her voice at home and even yelled at her boys. I've been living in such self-condemnation, because now that I've become the instant mother of two teenage sons (she had just married a widower in the church), I'm always yelling at home, and I guess I, too, believed that good Christian mothers just didn't do that. I had felt so defeated in my Christian life—until last week. For the first time, I didn't feel all alone."

Others agreed with what Jan was saying. Practically everyone had gotten some sort of blessing out of it, however unexpected. God had used the confrontation with Helen to speak to each of us. I silently asked Him to forgive me for having wanted to avoid what He had intended to use, just as I had before with Barbara Cole in the other group.

It hardly seemed possible that the three months of these second 3D groups were just about over. We decided to conclude by having a potluck dinner with all three groups together on the last Tuesday night. But as we were making plans and deciding what to ask everyone what to bring, we felt a check from the Lord. We listened, knowing that God was trying to get our attention about something. And what we felt was that we, the leaders, were to plan, cook and serve the meal. The dinner menu was to be a surprise for the 3Ders, and the whole occasion was to be an evening out for them. They loved the idea when we shared it with them.

"Dress up, and come prepared to celebrate," we announced. "We'll have a special last night together. "

And again without our realizing it, God was leading us, through this celebration, into a deeper awareness of a very important aspect of 3D: that the leaders were there for one purpose—to serve.

April 2 arrived, and it was a beautiful evening. The aroma of roasting beef filled the church, and it was the first thing we noticed the moment we opened the door. Ruth had shopped at the farmers' market for fresh vegetables and was readying platters of broccoli, cauliflower, and carrots. Potatoes were baked, then mashed and stuffed back in the shells with a little bit of grated cheese sprinkled on them. And for dessert we were having chilled cups of fresh fruit—diced apples, mixed with sliced peaches, fresh strawberries and blueberries and cantaloupe balls. We arranged it carefully so that it all looked as good as it smelled. A children's Sunday school classroom was somehow given the atmosphere of a private dining room, with crisp white tablecloths, and centerpieces of candles surrounded by arrangements of fresh-cut flowers, and other touches that came to us as we worked.

The women could hardly believe their eyes when they walked in! We suggested that they seat themselves next to someone from one of the other groups, rather than someone from their own group. There was no hesitation, and within minutes the room was filled with laughter and animated conversation.

We had invited Fred Schuman, an elder of the church and a good soloist, to help us with some special music. He did a fine job, and we were drawn together in song and then in sharing. The evening couldn't have been nicer, and the groups had a surprise for Dorcas and me. They presented us with lovely watches which, they told us, were symbolic of the time we had given them. We were deeply moved. The love of God permeated that evening from the beginning to the end.

What more could He do, I wondered. He had certainly blessed us in and through the 3D groups, even though we had never had any idea of where He was leading us. At this point, almost everyone in the three groups wanted to continue in 3D. And we decided that we would—but how it was going to work, or what we were going to do next, only God knew.

10

Learning to Receive

Outside the new social hall, I glanced at the coat rack and had to smile. There were hardly any coats there, even though it was still April and not what anyone would call a warm spring evening. Being a long-time dieter myself, I knew only too well the significance of shedding winter coats. The illusion that overweight people have—that a coat can hide twenty or twenty-five pounds—works the other way, as well. The successful dieter can't wait to get her winter coat put away. She'll take it off, usually too soon, and will shiver a little, if necessary, to show off her new figure.

Tonight was another orientation meeting, and again we had asked those 3Ders who wanted to continue, to come early. Most of them had lost a great deal of weight—hence the empty coat racks. Shivering a little myself, I went inside. There were thirty-four old 3Ders sitting in the rows, excited and eager to begin again. And by eight o'clock some thirty or so new women, a number of them with their coats still on, had come to hear about the program and ask questions.

"I can't believe this; I really can't believe it!" I kept saying to myself, and then remembered that I'd said the same thing three months before, at the beginning of 1974. "What is God doing?" I whispered to Dorcas.

"I haven't the vaguest idea," she replied, with a shrug, "but I guess we'd better get started."

We walked to the front of the room. I took a deep breath and said, "If we look shocked and surprised—and scared—it's because we are!" And from there, we let the Holy Spirit lead us in what to share, letting them know exactly what they were getting into, and how much it was going to involve, in terms of time and commitment. When everything we could think of was covered, several women who had completed their first three months spoke up.

Mary Doughty was the first to stand up, and I was surprised, because she had remained relatively quiet during most of the weeks the group had met. Nor had we felt any leading in that group to draw Mary out. She had cried almost every week, not that noticeably, but tears were falling continually. We sensed that those tears had something to do with the accidental death of her youngest son several months before, but we clearly felt the Holy Spirit saying, "Just let her cry. Those are tears of healing." And so we did. Tonight, apparently, she had decided to speak. The tears came again, before she could get the first words out, and then, "Most of you know that Tom and I lost our son Jim last October, very suddenly. . ." She cried some more, and someone handed her the Kleenex box. (We had learned to always have a box of Kleenex nearby.)

The room was perfectly still; you could feel people praying for Mary. It was extremely difficult for her to say what she wanted and needed to say, but she was determined to keep going. "It was an awful shock to us, but we did our best to accept it. We felt that, after all, God had allowed it to happen, and as Christians we were supposed to accept it and go on. Well, that sounds good, but the way I wound up handling my hurt was to eat every time I felt any grief, and in those first months, that was most of the time. In four months I had gained twenty-five pounds." She had regained her composure now and went on much more easily. "We had joined Parkminster only a few days before Jim died. Everyone was wonderful to us— friends at church and our family—and we wanted so much to have it all together for them. So we put on a victorious attitude when we went out, but in the privacy of our home we were crying lots."

I hurt, in my heart, as I listened to Mary. Many times I had been concerned about how she and Tom were doing, but each time I had seen them, they seemed so good that I had backed away from asking. I didn't want to bring up any unnecessary hurt by mentioning the whole thing. But now, listening to her, I realized how selfish I had been. I had chosen to believe what I had seen on the outside, and had not wanted to make even a suggestion that might have given them the opportunity to express the grief they were keeping bottled up.

"I joined 3D," Mary went on, "because I wanted to lose that weight, and I did. But that was only a small part of what happened to me. In 3D, I found that not only was it okay to cry in public, it was okay to hurt as a Christian, and it was okay to express that hurt to Christians. And once I was free to express some of that hurt, just by crying in my group, I began to experience God's healing deep inside." She smiled and said, "The twenty-five pounds were nothing more than stored-up tears that finally had a chance to come out." She hesitated. "You will never know," and here she sought the eyes of the others who had been in her group, "how much I appreciated your love and understanding, even though you never actually spoke to me about it. I think I know Jesus better now because of you."

She sat down with a big smile, and her eyes were sparkling. But there was hardly a dry eye in the room. Wiping the tears from my own eyes, I said, "Well, Mary, if shedding tears will take the pounds off, a lot of us are going to go home thinner tonight."

Testimony followed testimony after that—they were just popping up all over the room. And finally I had to step in and stop them, so we could get on with the meeting. The result of the evening was that sixty women signed up for 3D groups.

At the rate 3D was growing, all kinds of decisions were now necessary, and Bill suggested that we quickly get ourselves under the direction of the Session (the ruling board of a local Presbyterian church). And we did. By June of 1974, there were six 3D groups going simultaneously, and I was beginning to eat, sleep and even dream 3D, to the exclusion of all else— the dangerous exclusion of all else, though I didn't see that at the time.

Summer brought with it an opportunity for a complete change of pace, and I was delighted. Our new cottage on Cape Cod had been under construction since April and was at last nearing completion. We had decided to take three weeks of our August vacation a month early, in order to be able to work around the place and do some of the necessary jobs to make the cottage livable. And so, not long after the children finished school, we packed up and were off to Cape Cod. But what we had thought would be small finishing touches, like painting and varnishing, turned out to be considerably more than that. All the windows, inside and out, had to be either stained or painted—on both the first and second floors! We wanted the inside woodwork to remain natural, so three coats of polyurethane needed to be applied. And then there was the floor tile in the front hall, and the wallpapering we wanted in the kitchen and bathroom, and putting in a front lawn— if we had time. By the end of the three weeks we were less than half finished! Bill and I decided that the children and I should stay on for the remainder of the summer, and he would join us at the end of August.

I did little or no thinking about 3D during those busy summer months. In fact, the only time it came to mind was when a steady procession of visitors from Rochester kept appearing at the front door to visit and help. It was an unbelievable experience. Day after day, I would look out the window and see friends from church stopping out front. They knew I was there alone with the children and could use all the help I could get. We had room for the first few, but others camped down the road, and still others were staying at motels nearby. And in just about every case, it was a 3Der and her family.

Something else had happened during those nine months we had 3D groups. There was now a feeling of family and friends between us, instead of minister and parishioners. I loved having them drop in, and they got so much of the work done that there was little left for Bill to finish in August, and he was actually able to come and just relax for the last week of his vacation, rather than to work frantically to finish by Labor Day. But inevitably, with ten or twelve people living in an unfinished house with one bathroom, mixed in with the blessings were bound to be some times when our 3D experience of being open and honest with one another came in handy. There was, for instance, the time when Marilyn Christopher, the petite 3Der who had once been concerned about praying for forty women, arrived with her husband Bill and their four children—twin boys fourteen, a girl thirteen, and another ten. It happened that they were the church's wallpapering experts, and they heard we needed help to paper two rooms. They did a terrific job of wallpapering and put a lot of time into it, and I was very grateful. When the time came for them to begin their long trip home, I started making all sorts of plans for lunches for their trip, including baking some cookies and making fudge brownies and mixing up lots of lemonade.

"Oh, Carol, please don't," Marilyn said. "We were really looking forward to stopping on the way home."

"But," I insisted, "it will save lots of time and money to have a lunch with you." She was very insistent I not do it, but I was determined that I was going to do it, no matter what she said.

Finally, Marilyn raised her voice, and it was shaking. "Why can't you just once be on the receiving end! You do so much for all of us back at church, and for a change we have a chance to do something for you. But you won't let us!" She got up and walked out of the room, and so caught up was I in doing what I had planned on, that I still was unaware of how deeply she meant what she was saying. I continued setting out the necessary things to make the lunches. When she came back in and saw me, she burst out crying. "You didn't even listen to me, did you? We came, because we felt God wanted *us* to help *you!*"

It seemed to me she was making a very big deal out of nothing, but at last I stopped, to try to hear what she was saying.

"Why won't you just let us help you and stop insisting on outdoing us and giving back every way you can? We need to give, and you need to know how to receive." Suddenly, finally, I heard God speaking to me. And the only reason I could finally begin to hear Him, was because Marilyn had been willing to make a scene. Her honesty penetrated my massive insensitivity— of doing the "right thing" because it made me feel good.

All at once, I saw it and was stunned. I asked Marilyn to forgive me. Later, munching on one of the sandwiches I had made for them, I saw still more about why I was so compulsive about doing for others—indeed, why I was happiest when I was busy doing, doing, doing. It was another deeper level of my drive for acceptance. If I did enough for them, "they" (whoever "they" happened to be) would have to accept me. As I thought about that, I somehow saw that my lifelong scramble to do for others in order to be accepted, was going to have to stop. Now, I could start doing for others simply because God gave me the nudge, and it would be for His glory and not mine.

11

In Leading,
They were Led

"September 25th, 1974, 8:00 P.M." the announcement had read, and by eight, there were more than 150 women gathered at the church for our third orientation meeting. Word about 3D had spread all over the city, and women from many churches were there to hear about the new Christian diet program. And when we had finished laying it on the line—and we made very sure that no one was entering under any false conceptions—127 of them signed up.

The most immediate problem we faced was leadership. Figuring each team of leaders could lead two groups, that still meant we were going to need a dozen leaders. Where were we going to find them? After a lot of emergency praying, the solution we came up with was to approach those old 3D hands, whom God seemed to be saying were ready to assume the responsibility of group leadership. Almost to a woman, they protested, "Not me!" "But I still have so much to learn myself," Lois Pappa exclaimed. "And I have more weight to lose," moaned Helen McClurg in her new clear voice.

"I know, I know," I replied. "I felt exactly the same way, when I was asked to lead the first group. I wanted to be in a 3D group so I could get help, but God called me to assume the responsibility of leading the group, instead." I smiled. "I got more help than I expected—and not the way I thought it would come."

We talked a great deal about what a leader was supposed to be and what qualifications she should have. And we were reminded of the leaders whom God had called out from the beginning of time—weak and needy individuals, whose hearts were towards God and who loved Him. They were not persons of brilliance of mind or eloquent speech—Moses had a stuttering problem—but they were believers who were committed to serving God in any way that He called them to. "The essential qualification for leading people is still the same," I said smiling, "and that's a commitment to God and a willingness to serve Him wherever you are called. Are you willing?"

And so twelve old-timers took their places as 3D leaders, scared but willing to step out on faith. They were delighted that they could work in teams of two, rather than alone; and it made the call a good deal easier to accept. But, since the details of the program were still evolving week by week before our eyes, and we had no manual or instructions about how to conduct a successful 3D session, they were sent into groups dependent totally on God's guidance.

Dorcas and I continued to lead several groups, but increasingly we saw more clearly that our own call was evolving, too—to work more with the leaders themselves. They needed direction, encouragement, and counsel from us. And as we met with them weekly, we found our times of sharing together an invaluable experience. We were all growing in our relationship with the Lord, because He was demanding more from us than any of us felt equipped to handle. We didn't know how to lead leaders, and the leaders didn't know how to lead groups. So together we sought more of the wisdom and direction of God—watching as before our eyes, lives were being changed.

God was at work in all of us, and we knew it. We also began to come into some sense of the meaning of a "call" being for lay people, as well as ministers and missionaries. "You did not choose me, but I have chosen you. . ." (John 15:16) was a verse most of us thought belonged to the fulltime Christian worker only. Now we saw it was for us, too.

God's sense of humor also became apparent to all of us, as we worked together those next three months. It was uncanny how often the leaders would have in their particular group, not just one, but two or more persons with exactly the same problems they had. Thus, through their speaking up in the group to someone else, God spoke directly to their own hearts. Ruth Bailey found that she had a number of women who wanted to escape responsibilities and slip off to bed or a good "Christian" book. She had to speak strongly to them about being obedient to God, and in a couple of cases, she and her partner even helped them to get on a daily time schedule. She was able to speak with authority from her own experience, which now had become a tremendous asset. And each time, God turned the words right around and grounded them even deeper into her own life.

The same was true of Lois Pappa and Marilyn Christopher, who were both quiet in outward personality and who had several women in their group who simply refused to share of themselves. They saw how difficult it was for a group, when one or two people would steadfastly refuse to open up. And again, by encouraging others to share, they became even freer themselves.

God was working uniquely in the leaders, in a way most of them had not experienced before—in leading, they were being led.

Behind the scenes of 3D, God was giving Bill very definite teachings to be used in the groups, as well as key Scripture memory verses. We also were seeing the outlines for the members' disciplines. As each unfolded, we would type it up as fast as we could, run copies off, and pass them out in groups for weekly use. It was phenomenal, and we knew it was God, because the content was coming too quickly for it to be us. We made up Scripture verse cards to take home, found books and pamphlets to read, tapes to listen to, and even bought a second "gray monster" scale.

And for our expenses, we were now collecting a dollar per member per week. Someone was convicted that we needed to be disciplined in our finances, as well as our food, and we knew that was the word of God to us. With these funds, we bought tape recorders for group use, and Bill was then able to put the weekly teachings on tape, eliminating his need to be in every group.

Still the 3D program kept growing—nearly doubling in size, every time we opened it for new members. By spring of 1975, there were twenty-two groups meeting at Parkminster, and in addition, we had well over thirty leaders, necessitating several leaders' groups besides. A Free Methodist church in the community and also a Roman Catholic church were now asking if they could begin groups with our help, for which we were grateful, because every square inch of space at the church was being taken up by 3D groups, and we were having to turn people away.

Indeed, God was working in such a supernatural way through the expansion and growth of the 3D program, that I should have been watching a little more closely for the enemy of God to come sneaking up from behind. I had had more than one warning that things were getting out of kilter, but I had not listened. While on a retreat at the Community of Jesus, several people had remarked how much my life seemed to be wrapped up in 3D. Well, I thought to myself, of course it is. After all, there are over three hundred people involved in the program, and I am the one who bears the responsibility. They just didn't understand the demands and pressures that went along with running such a successful program.

Then, after the retreat was over, I sat down to talk with several of the women of the Community, who were direct and totally honest with me. "Frankly, Carol, you come on more like a career woman than a mother," one of them said. "And you seem unaware that your children need you to listen to them, just as much as the women in 3D." She went on to tell me that she had happened to notice Betsy, our eight-year-old daughter, approach me during afternoon coffee-hour the day before, very excitedly telling me about two twin sisters who were soon to arrive for a visit. "I don't think you even heard what she said, because your mind was on something else, and Betsy just wandered away, disappointed."

She was right. That was an exact replay of what had been happening at home all the time lately. The only thing on my mind for months had been 3D. I could not remember one significant thing that had happened for weeks to us as a family. It was devastating to me to realize this, and I broke down crying. I didn't have the slightest idea how I could get off this merry-go-round, but I wanted to.

Another woman from the Community spoke up and said that it wasn't the amount of time I was putting in on 3D; it was the attitude of my heart that was wrong. I wasn't sure what she meant by that, but I listened, They were so loving to me, and at the same time very honest. Yes, it stung—like mercurochrome on a cut. But that stinging meant that the possibility of subsequent infection, which would hurt far, far more, was being arrested. But typically, I wanted an instant solution. "What can I do? I'm overwhelmed with the responsibilities of 3D and my family. There just aren't enough hours in the day."

"Ask the Lord to help you," I was told. "You are taking

this 3D thing too much to yourself and not allowing God to carry the burdens and responsibilities."

I walked away from that discussion, feeling as I had when Cay and Judy talked to me about my being so critical. I didn't know how I was going to change, but three months afterwards, I knew I was less critical. And that reminded me of when Marilyn had told me how incapable I was of receiving from other people. In less than a year, I had learned more about myself and how I came across to others than I had learned over the previous twenty years.

Although I felt somewhat overwhelmed after this last confrontation, I knew it was absolutely right. So I began to try to forget 3D when I was home with the family. It helped, but I also sensed that while I was working hard to change my outside behavior again, there was more work necessary underneath. That, I had to leave to God. I couldn't change inside—that was His job. It would take time; I would have liked to have sat around and just waited until I was all perfect, but 3D and my family kept moving rapidly around me. So I asked God to make me more aware of the needs of my family, and I made an attempt at caring more for them at home and listening, especially to the children.

By May, 1975, 3D was blossoming in many of the churches around the area. A brief appearance on a nationally syndicated television talk show had deluged us with more than fifteen hundred letters of inquiry. Now we were known far beyond the immediate Rochester area, and all kinds of suggestions as to how to run the program better and what to do differently poured into the church office. Telephone calls were received from several different states, and people wanted help and counsel over the telephone and via the mail. It was incredible how many people, Christian people, were searching for help in these three areas of their lives—diet, discipline and discipleship.

The elders of the church decided to legally incorporate the program, appointing executive officers and a board of directors. "It is important that we follow and protect the direction in which God has been leading us," an elder said, "and not be tossed hither and yon by all these new suggestions."

He was right. We believed that God had been guiding us from the very beginning, and we did not want to lose the foundations He had laid. Some of the outside groups wanted more emphasis on the diet phase of the program, while others wanted to leave out the dieting and stress the spiritual disciplines more. And still others felt uncomfortable about any personal sharing or speaking truth in the groups, so they wanted this de-emphasized. It was sometimes hard to hear God amidst all these opinions.

In the meantime, as mute testimony to the effectiveness of the 3D program, with its strong emphasis on commitment, caring, openness and honesty, we were seeing more and more lives being rapidly and beautifully altered. We were also beginning to see the profound connection between the basic attitudes of members and their eating habits. All kinds and degrees of rebellion, fear, and anxiety were surfacing in the groups. Bubbling up everywhere were attitudes of self-pity, when people would not lose weight, and self-righteousness on the part of those who lost easily. We were indeed becoming the people God intended us to be—real, honest, and needy of a Savior to free us from ourselves.

We were also learning how to bring our poor attitudes into the light of God, there to confess them, and be forgiven so that we could move on. And to our utter astonishment, we lost a ton of weight in twelve weeks!

12

Stepping Out

"Carol, 3D is no longer God's answer to you; it has now become your answer to the hundreds of people involved in it," Judy Sorensen stopped and looked straight at me. "You're in danger of becoming a disciple of the 3D program, rather than a disciple of Jesus Christ."

Her words shook me. I had been making a real effort to care more for my family, and I had tried to unwrap myself as much as possible, whenever possible, from the demands of 3D, when they interfered with our home life. But Judy saw my problem differently. It was not something that I could just patch up with a few adjustments. She and Cay Andersen were in Rochester again, for another spring teaching mission at the church. It was May, 1975. And while they were delighted to see that the 3D program had grown so large so quickly, and that God was using it all over the area, they were concerned about where I was spiritually. All week, during the mission, they had seen me running around, directing 3D leaders, hurrying in and out of groups and so on.

Cay joined the conversation. "Whenever God is doing a work in the hearts and lives of people, be on guard for the big self moving into God's place. Only God is allowed at the center of His work," she paused. "So, Carol, step out."

115

"Step out? You mean step out of 3D?" I asked in a barely audible voice.

"Oh, no," she chuckled, "just out of God's place at the center."

She made it sound so easy. In fact, to graphically demonstrate, she actually took a big step to the right of where she had been standing in Bill's office. "Just like this, out of the way so God can get back in where He belongs." She laughed, but I couldn't; I wanted to quit the whole thing. I had been trying so hard since the woman at the Community spoke to me about my career-woman attitude. And evidently, it hadn't done a bit of good.

"Don't be so discouraged with yourself," she went on, "That's our sin nature, to move in on God's territory, and it's a continuing battle."

It seemed like a losing battle to me. But even in the midst of their strong warning to me, I saw the love of God again. This whole journey with my weight and my need for various disciplines was so that Jesus Christ might be glorified by my life. And I had slipped off course again. I had confused God's work with God Himself. I knew in my heart that I had lost a great deal of closeness to Him, and I knew it because I was so caught up in all the nuts-and-bolts details of the organizational needs of 3D. I wasn't peaceful. And I had no joy. It was work, work, work.

And so, on that May afternoon, Cay and Judy spoke the words that God wanted me to hear. I couldn't keep from crying. The words had pierced my heart and soul. "How do I get out of the center of it?" I asked through my tears.

"By an act of your will and with the help of God," Judy answered. "That's where it has to begin."

As they spoke further to me, the picture became clearer and clearer. I had closed out the rest of the life at church. There was no time to go to Bible study or circle meetings. All those 3D groups meeting each week in the church, plus several in other churches in the community and then the leadership responsibility for thirty leaders at Parkminster and ten or twelve others at Holy Ghost Church—there was no time, no time for anything but 3D! I didn't ask Bill much about anything else in the church. But instead, every time I got him to myself, I would pour a million questions on him—about 3D. Oh yes, I did shut it off, as best I could, at home with the children, but the minute they were out of my sight, I was chin deep in it again.

Suddenly, the smile face popped into my mind. Only the words beneath it read differently now: "Smile, Carol has the answer!" I felt sick.

"How could I?" I moaned, and I made myself tell them what had just come into my mind.

"What did you expect from a sinner?" Cay laughed again, and her laugh was warm and contagious.

I knew she wasn't making light of what I was seeing but she was trying to help me get into reality and not go down in anguish and depression about the whole thing.

"Just go off by yourself," Judy suggested, "and give the whole program back to God and take your rightful position under Him."

I just wanted to sit there and cry. And again I had the feeling that in ten or fifteen minutes they had taken care of something that I thought would require at least a couple of hours.

"There's no one in the chapel now, so why don't you go down by yourself and talk it out with the Lord. And you can cry all you want! Only be sure those are tears of repentance and not self-pity," Judy cautioned.

Someone had once told me the difference between those two kinds of tears, and I had never forgotten it. "Tears of self-pity will only take you down into depression, while tears of repentance will take you out into life and joy."

Bill had been sitting very quietly beside me, not saying a word. But when I made no move to leave, he got up and opened the door of his office and said sternly, "Be obedient, Carol. The chapel's free and we'll see you in a while."

I really wanted him to go with me. The last thing I wanted was to be alone now. I had no idea why, until I closed the door behind me in the chapel and knelt at the altar. Then it came to me. It had been so long since I had come to God alone and in need, that I had forgotten how to be in need and helpless before a Holy God. I had been using God every day to help me to be strong and have the wisdom and understanding to guide those entrusted to my care. I had been praying faithfully for my family and all thirty leaders, but I had forgotten much about my daily need of a Savior to save me from myself.

Sobbing as I knelt at that little altar, looking straight at the shiny gold cross, I saw my tear-stained face in it. It was a tired, hurt, strained face. I cried, "God, come close to me. I need you so much." But He seemed far from me.

I don't know how long I knelt and cried that afternoon, but it was an experience I'll never forget. Slowly, ever so slowly, as I looked at the cross, the reflection of my face disappeared. At first, it had been like a mirror instead of a cross. All I could see was me. Then the cross became more evident to me in its wholeness. And I began to feel the unexplainable presence of God. And the pain and hurt and disappointment began to lift. I knew it was going to be okay. God was now again moving into the center of my life. It felt good.

It was through that experience, that the third D of the 3D program took on a much greater significance to me. God had personally walked me through the defeat and discouragement of a weight problem into some semblance of victory, so that I could share with others. Then He had been teaching me a great deal about the amazing freedom that comes through

discipline. And now I had touched on the very core of it all—
what it really meant to be a disciple of Jesus Christ.

I had deceived myself into thinking that because it was
Christian work that I was so deeply involved in, God was
automatically at the center. It was a mistake I had made over
and over again in my Christian life. But many of the things
I had done in the name of Christ, I now saw were centered
around me, not Him. And God blessed them anyway, in spite
of me. But now He was beginning to show me what it meant
to be His disciple.

Things were different after that. I finally understood what
the Community women had meant when they told me, "It isn't
the amount of time you are giving to 3D; it's your heart attitude
that is wrong."

I had to laugh; it was so simple. There was room for only
one of us, Him or me, at the center of 3D, and as long as
I was occupying that place, He was not about to. As much
as my ego might have wanted to remain there, I really wanted
Him there, not me. And so, by His grace and mercy, I was
able to take that giant step that Cay Andersen had talked about.
And, funny thing: when I stepped out of the center, I found
I was stepping into Christ.

Epilogue

On this beautiful summer day in 1998, I look back to the day in August of 1973 when God touched my heart with the concept of a small group centered on diet, discipline and discipleship. With great joy I find that 3D continues to be an answer to prayer for women and men across the world who struggle not only with weight but with many other aspects of their lives that need the touch of God. The 3D program has been used in every one of the United States, in every province of Canada, and in more than twenty other countries.

For many years the 3D program occupied almost all my time. I spoke to groups all across North America and was interviewed on hundreds of radio and television programs. At the same time, for over 17 years my husband and I served a church in Rochester, New York, where the 3D groups began. Over those years the children you have met in this book grew to adulthood. Our last child, Helen, who missed the pages of this book, is herself now the mother of three.

After our years in Rochester, my husband and I moved to the Community of Jesus, on Cape Cod, Massachusetts, where the beginnings of 3D were nurtured. The 3D program continued to grow as the Christian publisher Paraclete Press took on the distribution of the 3D materials. I now serve as director of marketing at Paraclete Press, and although my time is no longer entirely filled with the 3D program, it is still a tremendous part of my life.

After twenty-five years it is more than obvious to me that God raised up the 3D program, through many miracles leading us in the right direction. The program remains true to its beginnings. We have never said that being thin was the answer to life's problems. What we have always done is encourage people to share their lives in small groups, to read and memorize the Scriptures, and to develop the discipline of a daily prayer time—and these principles are still the very foundation of 3D. God has raised up other Christian diet programs since the beginning of the 3D program, and I have no doubt that He will bless and use them. But I also have no doubt that His hand of blessing abides on 3D—and I believe that thousands more will find help through Diet, Discipline and Discipleship.